A WORLD TRANSFORMED

A World Transformed

EXPLORING THE SPIRITUALITY
OF MEDIEVAL MAPS

Lisa Deam

CASCADE *Books* · Eugene, Oregon

A WORLD TRANSFORMED
Exploring the Spirituality of Medieval Maps

Copyright © 2015 Lisa Deam. All rights reserved. Except for brief quotations in critical publications or reviews, no part of this book may be reproduced in any manner without prior written permission from the publisher. Write: Permissions, Wipf and Stock Publishers, 199 W. 8th Ave., Suite 3, Eugene, OR 97401.

Cascade Books
An Imprint of Wipf and Stock Publishers
199 W. 8th Ave., Suite 3
Eugene, OR 97401

www.wipfandstock.com

ISBN 13: 978-1-62564-283-7

Cataloging-in-Publication data:

Deam, Lisa

    A world transformed : exploring the spirituality of medieval maps / Lisa Deam.

    xvi + 142 p. ; 23 cm. —Includes bibliographical references.

    ISBN 13: 978-1-62564-283-7

    1. Geography, Medieval—Maps. 2 Spiritual life. I. Title.

BX2435 .D41 2015

Manufactured in the U.S.A.

Chapter 8 contains passages that originally appeared in the Trinity 2011 issue of *The Cresset*. Reprinted with permission.

Chapter 9 contains passages that originally appeared in the Lent 2009 issue of *The Cresset*. Reprinted with permission.

Scripture taken from the Holy Bible, NEW INTERNATIONAL VERSION®, NIV® Copyright © 1973, 1978, 1984, 2011 by Biblica, Inc.® Used by permission. All rights reserved worldwide.

Soli Deo gloria

Contents

Illustrations

Acknowledgments

The medieval world maps that form the subject of this book were made some seven hundred years ago. Sometimes I think my book has itself been in formation for about that long. The idea was born during my graduate studies at the University of Chicago, nourished in the Lilly Fellows Program at Valparaiso University, where I first began to consider the spiritual implications of medieval maps, and came to fruition—appropriately, given the subject matter—when I decided to strike out on a new path in life.

Writing was a spiritual discipline that brought much joy. I cherished the hours of reflection and solitude that brought the book about. Yet I did not write it alone. Participants in mapping workshops I led raised questions, made observations, and responded enthusiastically to medieval maps, all of which shaped my thinking. My friend and colleague Julie Straight thoughtfully critiqued a good bit of material in the book. I would not be the writer I am today without her. James Old, editor of *The Cresset*, where two chapters of the book were originally published, also provided much-appreciated editorial support. I also owe a debt of gratitude to readers of early versions of the book: Alan Farhi, Mary McQueen, Dawn Wheat, and especially Ailisha O'Sullivan, who encouraged me to fearlessly explore the darker aspects of maps and faith. On the other side of darkness lies redemption.

My appreciation goes to Jeanie Hoover, Susie Hord, Preston Yancey, and Charlie Collier, my editor at Wipf and Stock, for helping me think through important issues in the book, and to Margriet Hoogvliet for continuing conversations amidst a friendship that was born over medieval maps.

This book would be of little value without the illustrations. The institutions and individuals I contacted for assistance were wonderful to work with. They are credited in the List of Illustrations, but I would like to thank them here: artist Spencer Sauter; Professor Daniel Terkla; artist

Justin Vining; Hereford Cathedral; The British Library; The New York Public Library; and The Harry Ransom Center at the University of Texas at Austin. Special thanks go to Margriet Hoogvliet, University of Groningen, Gerda Huisman, Special Collections of the University Library Groningen, and Bernard Bousmanne and Ann Kelders of the Royal Library of Belgium; Drs. Bousmanne and Kelders also have my enduring gratitude for facilitating my introduction, when I was a graduate student, to medieval maps via the manuscripts that housed so many of them.

The editorial and design teams at Wipf and Stock provided much support and expertise in bringing the book, with its many illustrations, to publication.

My greatest thanks and admiration go to my family and especially my husband, Forrest Christian, without whose editorial insights and tireless support this book could not have been written. I am grateful to be walking the map with him.

FIGURE 1. The Hereford Map, ca. 1300.

FIGURE 2. The Ebstorf Map, ca. 1300.

FIGURE 3. The Psalter Map, ca. 1265.
© The British Library Board, Add. MS 28681, fol. 9r.

1

Introduction: A Spiritual GPS

At the end of my sophomore year in college, the time came to choose my major. Up to that point, I was one of the few, the proud, the undeclared. Based on the classes I enjoyed the most, I had winnowed my options to art history or religion. Little did I know that by choosing art history, I'd be getting both.

To be precise, I'd be getting Jesus. As I settled into my art history studies, I found myself going back in time—from my first love, the Hudson River School, I traveled back to the Italian Renaissance and finally landed in the Middle Ages, never to depart this monstrous and marvelous era. I tried to look at the array of images I encountered—the stained glass and manuscripts, sculpture and panel paintings—with a scholarly eye, since that was expected of me. I soon discovered, however, that there was really no way to separate medieval art from medieval faith and spirituality—and from my own faith. I loved the way that medieval artists saw their world: with creativity and in intimate connection with the creator. It became the way I see my own world, or the way I try to see it.

One image in particular changed my view of the world. At the beginning of my dissertation research, I encountered the Hereford Map, one of the treasures of medieval art and culture (fig. 1). Made in England around the year 1300, this map portrays the world as it was known in the High Middle Ages. It transformed not only the course of my scholarly career but also my journey with God.

At first glance, the Hereford Map does not seem capable of guiding anyone's journey. Geographically, it is completely foreign to our modern eyes. It pictures a world before the age of exploration, a world that took its shape more from tradition and lore than from science or empirical observation. The Hereford Map pictures the world as a circle, a little over four feet in diameter, in which nestle closely together the three inhabited continents of Europe, Africa, and Asia. The River Ocean surrounds these land masses, creating a single, continuous coastline that girds the world. The map is oriented to the east rather than the north, so that Asia, the largest continent, tops the earth. To see the world as we are accustomed, we have to turn the map sideways. Even then, nothing is very recognizable.

If we look at this foreign world with the eyes of our faith, however, we begin to find some familiar landmarks. Along the Mediterranean Sea, we see a small portrait of Saint Augustine, bishop of Hippo in the fifth century, whose autobiography, *The Confessions*, has guided so many in their spiritual journey through the world. Augustine stands in profile before a church portal, wearing his bishop's miter (fig. 4).

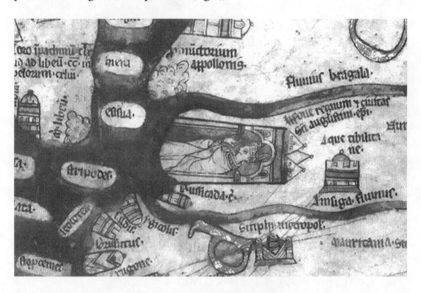

FIGURE 4. Augustine, Bishop of Hippo. Detail from the Hereford Map.

At the top of the map, and further back in time, the drama of creation is played out in the circular, walled Garden of Eden. Adam and Eve take the forbidden fruit, and the journey of humanity begins.

The Hereford Map features many other sites from the history of Christianity. Some of them may not seem particularly significant to us but were certainly important to the map's original viewers. In the medieval era, the map was displayed in Hereford Cathedral, and the city of Hereford itself is proudly featured in England, in the northwest corner of the world. Rome, the head of the church, and Paris, home to a university known for its school of theology, also receive a place of prominence on the map.

But there is more. Above all these earthly sites, the Jesus of eternity sits in majesty, overseeing and judging his creation. And in the precise center of the creation lies Jerusalem, the city in which the historical Jesus died and rose again. On the map, Jerusalem appears as a circular, walled city from which rises a ghostly image of the crucifixion.

The Hereford Map thus encompasses the history of the world from the creation to the day of judgment, all while centering on the beating heart of our faith—Jesus Christ. In this image of a Christ-centered world are lessons for our world today. We will find not just history lessons or lessons in Christian doctrine, although the map does teach us about these topics. More importantly, the Hereford Map provides lessons in seeing our world transformed by Jesus. When medieval Christians came face to face with the map, they saw their world, including the everyday places in which they lived and worked, in intimate connection with the God of history and creation. We can learn to see our world this way, too. We have a place on the map!

A World We Crave

The Hereford Map shows a world we need, a world we desperately crave. As Christians, we long to see our everyday world in intimate connection with God. We want to walk more closely with the creator. We strive for this all our life. Yet our walk, as we well know, is not always straightforward. It is easy to feel lost in the world. Sometimes we lose sight of God in the landscape of our life. We wonder where he is in our times of trouble or how our faith matters in our secular workplace.

A few years ago, my Bible study group did a lesson on time management. We discussed godly ways to spend time and came to the conclusion that God cares about everything we do, from physical exercise to relationships to jobs and careers. We agreed that God is at the center of all our activities. But evidently, a key piece of the time puzzle was still missing. Toward the end of the lesson, my friend Michael, who is a very fine interior designer, threw his hands in the air and exclaimed, "Well, okay, but I still don't see what furniture has to do with my faith!" Michael's faith was real. Yet he had trouble seeing God in certain parts of his life. He didn't really need a lesson in "time management." He needed to know that his faith mattered.

I sympathize with Michael. There have been times when I, too, have thrown up my hands in frustration. I used to believe that, as a Christian, I should not be attending graduate school, studying medieval maps, or devoting my time to research and writing. What does faith have to do with all that? Does any of it matter to God? I struggled through several years of guilt and confusion. The maps themselves showed me a way out of this morass. I finally realized that the maps I was studying pictured not only the history of salvation for the benefit of medieval pilgrims. They also pictured *my* history and *my* salvation. I had a place in their beautiful, Christ-centered world.

So do we all. This book, born from my studies and my groping, imperfect faith, is for Michael and for me and for every Christian who wants to see more of God in her world. I wrote it because sometimes we feel lost on our journey of faith: we need to pause, pull over to the side of the road, and reach for a map to guide us. In this book, I am going to suggest that we reach for the Hereford Map. This map, which pictures the creation transformed by the presence of God, teaches us to find our place in the world. If we heed the map's lessons, we can learn to see our ordinary lives inscribed in God's plan of redemption that was set in place at the beginning of time. Our faith matters. So do our jobs, our struggles, and all the mundane hours that make up our days. They are an integral part of an incredible, Christ-centered world.

It is no small thing to find our spiritual journey written into the history of the world. It reassures those of us who feel lost or who want to deepen our faith beyond the Sunday school lessons we hear in church. "Perhaps somewhere in the subterranean chambers of your life you have heard the call to deeper, fuller living," writes Richard Foster in his influential book on the spiritual life, *Celebration of Discipline.*[1] Have you heard this call? Do you long to experience a deeper, more vibrant faith? A faith that matters? If so, medieval world maps are for you. They can help you more fully live out your faith by showing you your place in the overarching story of creation, sin, and salvation. This is our story, but it is not one that we always hear. In an effort to be relevant to modern life, many churches today have cut themselves loose from history—the history of Christianity and the history of salvation itself. As a result, we have a heightened awareness of *our* story

1. Foster, *Celebration*, 2.

4

and *our* needs and a far dimmer grasp of the story God is telling about the world. Yet I can think of nothing more relevant than understanding our role in God's divine plan. We are relevant—cherished, significant—to the creator of the universe. And we can learn to live as though we are.

We need the vision of history shown on medieval maps to deepen our sense of belonging in God's world. We need the testimony of medieval Christians who help us learn to think about our faith this way. If we are overly worried about the question of relevance, we can bring the Hereford Map into the twenty-first century by comparing it to the maps we use all the time. Most of us would never dream of taking a journey, at least a long and complicated one, without the aid of a map. We rely on maps to show us where we are and to get us where we need to go. Shouldn't we do the same on our spiritual journey?

But, come to think of it, most of us do not use maps at all. Gone are the days of wrestling with unwieldy paper creations that can never again be folded into their original form! Today we use positioning systems and devices, such as mobile apps and GPS units. We program and interact with them. Sometimes, we talk to them. Perhaps we can think of the Hereford Map as an app for our time. In this map, and others from the medieval era, we find a spiritual GPS for our journey with God. It is fully programmable, highly interactive, and will get us where we need to go. It will take us to the heart of our faith and help us travel in a world centered on Jesus Christ.

Going Medieval

I love telling people that my spiritual map is medieval. It raises some eyebrows. It elicits chuckles. Sometimes, it worries people. In popular culture, the Middle Ages has not been able to entirely shake off its reputation as the "dark ages." When I first began thinking about the concept for this book, a pop song climbed the charts. I can't quote some of its lyrics in polite company, but one line in the song goes, "your point of view is medieval." It's not meant as a compliment. But when directed at me, I take it as such. My point of view *is* medieval—it's terribly old-fashioned, dredged up from the musty libraries and churches of a bygone era.

My musty point of view relieves me of a great burden. I don't have to reinvent my faith; I don't have to think of anything new to say. When I pull out my pictures of maps to show anyone who is willing to look, I am drawing on the wisdom of medieval Christians who, some seven hundred years ago, painted a glorious picture of Jesus Christ centering the world in which they lived.

Like many things that have gone out of fashion, the medieval world-view is so old that it's new again. It speaks to us as surely as it spoke to the people who made and viewed this vision of the world. I am far from the first person to discover the wisdom of the Middle Ages, of course. Whatever its reputation in popular culture, the medieval era has been staging a spiritual comeback for some time. Too many Christians, as I intimated above, are hearing the message that the past is not relevant to their faith. Others are discovering the value of medieval practices such as praying the hours, going on pilgrimage, and walking the labyrinth. They take a confessional journey with Saint Augustine or order their days according to the rule of Saint Benedict. They find in these historical figures and practices a way to live out their faith and to connect with their spiritual heritage.

I am often surprised—and delighted—by the resurgences of medieval spirituality that I encounter in contemporary culture. My hometown, a smallish Midwestern city, has no fewer than three labyrinths, with another outside of town, that echo the great labyrinth in the medieval cathedral of Chartres. In these places of peace, people take a journey that Christians have been taking for hundreds of years. It is a journey to the centering presence of Christ, much as medieval maps picture a world with the cross of Christ at its center.

I love these labyrinths and maps because I am a medieval junkie. I often go about with my head in the clouds of the past—right around the year 1300. Yet the medieval era has much to teach all Christians, not just the history-obsessed. We merely need to be ready to learn—to open our minds and travel to the past in search of God. When we do, we will find ideas and practices that can transform our faith. In many cases, these practices fill a need in our life or correspond to ways we are already trying to live. In medieval labyrinths and pilgrimage routes, for example, we learn about our lifelong route to and with Jesus. In fixed-hour prayer, we see our need to turn to God throughout the day.

To these practices we can add the world-altering vision of medieval maps. In fact, maps might be said to sum up the worldview of the Christian Middle Ages. The medieval desire to see life in intimate connection with God finds its fullest expression on the maps that show Jesus at the center of creation, history, and daily life. Medieval Christians were no better than the rest of us, and I do not mean to idealize this time period or the people who lived in it. Yet, just as one flawed person can help another, medieval Christians give us a gift in their maps. They teach us to see our own journey taking place in a Christ-centered world. This is why my point of view is medieval. It is why the Middle Ages is a worthy destination for time-traveling Christians today.

Learning from Medieval Maps

While many Christians know what a labyrinth is or perhaps have visited other medieval monuments, such as monasteries and cathedrals, few can name or call to mind a medieval map. Thus far, maps have remained mostly the preserve of scholars. This is a shame, because the maps contain much to delight the eye and the mind. In fact, perusing a medieval map is like taking a crash course in medieval life and thought. These maps reward the time spent looking at them. And they do take some time. The Hereford Map alone has over one thousand inscriptions and a similar number of painted scenes and symbols. It is truly an encyclopedia of medieval life and culture. On this map, we see the ordinary world in which Europeans lived and conducted their affairs, foreign lands they visited or feared, and the history in which they saw their own age unfolding. The more exotic sights on the map, such as the unusual creatures in medieval Africa, are perhaps the most eye-catching, but I also love the ordinary places—the cities and trade routes and even the good places to eat, such as "fat Bologna" (Italian food for dinner, anyone?). I sometimes think of these as snapshots (if I can borrow a term from the age of photography), and I value them because they remind me that real people viewed these maps—people who, like me, had things to do, a day to get through, a life to live.

We will explore many of these exotic and everyday sites in the course of this book. As we do, we will find the Hereford Map to be a delight to the soul as well as the eye. As we learn about the medieval view of the world, we learn about walking the world with God. The maps' geographical sites are windows into not only medieval life but also medieval spirituality. In addition to some of the practices I mentioned above, such as pilgrimage and prayer, medieval maps teach us about less familiar spiritual principles. We find on the Hereford Map, for example, lessons not only in physical pilgrimage but also pilgrimage of the heart. On another map of the era, we learn about the tender experience of Jesus as mother. Above all, these maps teach us about the practice of centering on Christ. These and other facets of medieval spiritual life can inform our journey.

Taking a medieval map on a journey of faith is not without its difficulties. We know what is on the maps but so little about who made them and how they were used. A book about maps, therefore, is not going to be a book about spiritual heroes, no matter how much supporting material is included. As I write about medieval maps and try to tease out their spiritual principles, I can't rely on the force of personality. There is no biography, either of the maps' artists or their users.

Take the Hereford Map, for example. Probably more has been written on the mystery of this map's origin than on any other issue regarding it. A legend in the lower left corner of the map reads, "Let all who have this history—or who shall hear, or read, or see it—pray to Jesus in his divinity to have pity on Richard of Holdingham, or of Sleaford, who made it and laid it out, that joy in heaven may be granted to him." This legend seems to name the map's maker. But we can't be sure whether the legend means that Richard made the map or whether he was the patron who provided for its creation. Scholars don't even know *which* "Richard of Holdingham" the legend references. According to some historians, it refers to three separate people named Richard, all of whom collaborated on the map!

Yet the legend does tell us something concrete. It asks for prayer. "Let all who have this history [i.e., this map] pray to Jesus in his divinity." It begs divine mercy on behalf of the person (or persons) in some way responsible for the map's two thousand pictures and inscriptions. The map, in other words, makes a spiritual demand on the people who looked at it.

And we know that the people who viewed the map were likely to be praying people: they were pilgrims. Shortly after its creation, the map was displayed in Hereford Cathedral, a major pilgrimage site in western England, near the Welsh border. The cathedral housed two shrines, those of Saint Ethelbert and Saint Thomas Cantilupe. Saint Thomas was canonized in 1320, a few years after the Hereford Map was made, and his tomb enjoyed popularity in the first part of the fourteenth century. Ordinary people as well as nobles came to seek healing and give thanks for cures received.

Scholars used to believe that the map formed the central part of an altarpiece in the cathedral. That viewpoint has mostly been discredited. But that it hung somewhere in the cathedral seems likely. Historians now propose that it graced the same chapel or transept that housed the tomb of

Saint Thomas. Pilgrims to the cathedral would have come face to face with the map, as visitors to Hereford Cathedral do today.

Thus we know two things about how the Hereford Map might have been used. It encouraged prayer, and it was viewed by pilgrims—people on a spiritual journey. This may not seem like much to go on, but I think it forms a good starting point. It tells us that we are on the right track in treating medieval maps as images for spiritual meditation. Augustine wrote, "The circle of the earth is our great book. In it I read the perfection which is promised in the book of God."[2] As circles of the earth, maps could be contemplated in the same way that a sacred text might be parsed, studied, and taken to heart. The Hereford Map's legend calls it a "history," which brings to mind an account like a chronicle.

Now, looking at a map is not exactly like perusing a text—I am trained as an art historian and, with apologies to Augustine, I believe that a picture communicates in different ways than a text. While we can liken medieval maps to texts, we might also compare them to sacred images, such as icons. The maps reward close looking and prolonged viewing. We circle the world with our eyes, making new connections and discovering new sights and insights. I've been looking at the Hereford Map for years, and sometimes it still surprises me with something new. It has been difficult to resist the impulse to rewrite all the chapters in this book based on my ongoing discoveries.

The best discoveries are the spiritual ones. Sometimes, as if following the instructions on the map's legend, I am led to pray. Seeing Jesus at the center of the world, I exalt the God of creation. Or I cry out to him for help. I find guidance in this spiritual roadmap in which all paths point to Jesus.

Programming Our Spiritual GPS

I have learned to let go of my scholarly frustrations concerning the Hereford Map's origins and to trust my response to the world it portrays. This book, in fact, represents my shift from viewing medieval maps as a scholar to viewing them as someone on a spiritual journey. From a spiritual vantage point, the mystery of the map's creation can be a virtue. Rather than pointing to any one person, the map seems to capture the spirit of an age—one that reaches out to our age. The image of a Christ-centered world is exactly what we need in our topsy-turvy world.

2. Augustine, *Epistulae*, 107. English translation in Mittman, *Maps and Monsters*, 31.

So let's program our spiritual GPS and see where it takes us. Let's look at the way medieval Christians saw their world—and find guidance for our own. Each chapter in this book explores a geographical feature of medieval maps and relates it to our walk of faith. The chapters are grouped into sections that tell us about *finding* Christ in our world, *journeying* with him, and *being* in his presence. The maps are able to teach us these things because their features are not only geographical but spiritual and historical as well. The centrality of Jerusalem, for example, was taken as a geographical fact in the Middle Ages. However, the city of Jerusalem as pictured on the Hereford Map also visualized the primacy of Jesus Christ in God's plan of salvation and was the endpoint of the most important pilgrimage route in the Middle Ages. Consequently, we will look at medieval Jerusalem from several angles in this book. One chapter helps us learn to center our own world on Christ; another describes the heart's journey to Jerusalem each day. We will also look at the edge of the medieval world, a place that symbolized physical and spiritual wilderness. From the edge, we learn to see Jesus in the dark corners of our world. As we go from the center to the edge and every place in between, we will learn to walk the medieval world and so to walk our world with God.

For me, the primary value in this walk of faith lies in the help it provides in the difficulties of life. I have always been one to ask the big questions. Why is life, even the Christian life, so hard? Will I be able to persevere? What do I do when, as so often happens, I lose sight of God? Medieval maps speak to these questions. They provide reassurance that God is in control, and they challenge me to order my world around him. They also suggest simple practices to reorient me when I am feeling lost. These practices are included at the end of each chapter.

When I first began studying medieval art, I learned about a popular spiritual practice, praying the hours. Using small prayer books, or books of hours, lay Christians could pray their way through the day. (We know of at least two prayer books that contained maps, incidentally. We will look at one of them later in this book.) I was especially taken by the title of an exhibition catalogue of books of hours in the Walters Art Gallery: *Time Sanctified*. For me, this title captured the notion that time, something we all experience, can be touched by God and made divine. Ordinary life can be transformed.

Medieval maps show the world transformed. They give us a picture of a world in which Jesus Christ is an active presence; he is shaping history, he is shaping the hours of the day, and he is shaping the journey of his people. With medieval maps as our guide, we can walk this world. It does not mean that our problems will magically disappear. Far from it. Our world will always have its moments of danger and tedium, its unknowns and uncertainties. But we can learn to see Jesus in them. We can find practices and paths by which to navigate all the territories of our life.

I invite you to travel these paths with me. Together, we will be pilgrims on a journey. When we take out our medieval map and hit the road, we will find that Jesus takes our ordinary world and transforms it into something extraordinary.

2

Finding Christ at the Center

I always find it fascinating when a work of art reveals something about the way it was made. In a Rembrandt painting, for example, globs of paint ride the surface of the canvas, revealing each dab and stroke of the master's brush. Paintings in medieval manuscript books, by contrast, can be so transparent that the artist's preliminary sketch peeps out from under the surface. In both cases, we see a bit of the creative process at work.

Medieval maps sometimes reveal their making, too. In the center of the Hereford Map, there is a small pinprick or hole that is clearly visible to the naked eye (as long as you are close enough to the map to see it). Scholars believe that this rupture in the parchment marks the spot on which the mapmaker anchored his compass as he drew the circumference of the earth. Given the map's four-foot diameter, that must have been some compass!

This small record of the map's making has a great deal of meaning. The little pinprick lies in the exact center of the world. And there, in that spot, an artist drew the city of Jerusalem. Above the city, another artist sketched in a small picture of the crucifixion (fig. 5). We can almost compare the hole in the parchment to the holes in Christ's hands, feet, and sides as he is nailed to the cross. The map's makers may not have thought of the pinprick in this way, but they certainly knew the significance of Jerusalem. With their pinprick and picture, they were following a time-honored tradition that placed this most sacred of cities in the center of the inhabited world.

What a beautiful way to make a map! Begin with the cross. Let Jerusalem shape the contours of the earth. The map's making contains an echo of what God did in the beginning, creating the world and ordering it around his son.

FIGURE 5. City of Jerusalem at the center of the Hereford Map. Although the map is degraded in this area, a picture of the crucifixion can be seen rising from the city.

It also leads to questions about our world. Each day, we give shape to our world through our beliefs and our way of life. What does our world look like? Does it begin with the cross? Is it given form and coherence by Jesus Christ? Or has it begun to lose the perfect shape the creator gave it? These are challenging questions, even for Christians. So many things clutter our world—so many distractions, competing beliefs, and false promises— that Jesus sometimes gets crowded out. We forget the place that he once occupied in our lives, the passion that we once had for him. Our world may no longer be recognizable to us.

Maybe it's time to reshape our world. Time to order it, chart it, plot its contours anew. To do so, we need to think like cartographers of old. We need to think medieval. That is the task of the present chapter. As we become familiar with medieval maps, we will discover how mapmakers saw their world, especially its sacred center. In the process, we may get the urge to become cartographers, too. By chapter's end, we may find ourselves pulling out our own compass and redrawing our little world.

A Question of Belief

When I speak on the topic of medieval maps, I am usually asked whether mapmakers (and map users) really believed that Jerusalem lay at the center of the world. I have a difficult time answering this question. The quick answer is yes. The centrality of Jerusalem was indeed taken as a given for much of the Middle Ages. Texts cite it as fact. Maps show it as truth. Still, to those of us living in the modern age, it seems a rather untenable way of picturing the world.

If we look closely at the shape and organization of the medieval world, the centrality of Jerusalem becomes more understandable. In the year 1300, the world was smaller than it is today. We should remember that the Hereford Map was made nearly two centuries before the voyages of Columbus. Consequently, the Middle Ages knew only three continents: Europe, Africa, and Asia. Some maps hinted at other landmasses, but they remained shadowy. Most maps stuck with the continents known to be inhabited.

On medieval maps, the three continents lie close together and are divided by bodies of water. The small map pictured in figure 6 provides a good illustration. In the lower half of the world, the Mediterranean Sea separates Europe from Africa. On the right, the Nile River divides Africa and Asia, and on the left, the Don River (along with the Aegean Sea) divides Europe and Asia. Together, these bodies of water form a "T" shape inscribed within the circular boundary of the world ("O"). Appropriately, these maps are known as T-O maps today. Some of the simplest T-O maps portray the outline of the three continents and little else. Others are quite elaborate. The Hereford Map is a T-O map, a very complex one in which the continents have been filled in with thousands of geographical and historical details.

A world shaped like an O seems to cry out for a center. And medieval mapmakers gave it one—right at the crossing of the T, at the place where the three continents meet. Here, beginning in the thirteenth century, they placed the city of Jerusalem. One of the largest T-O maps from the Middle Ages centers on Jerusalem, as does one of the smallest. All in all, we can

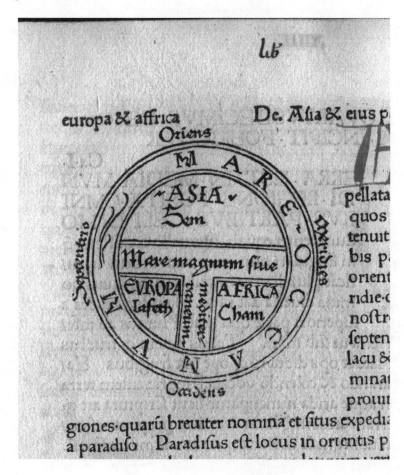

FIGURE 6. Printed T-O map, 1472

point to a group of about fourteen medieval maps that place Jerusalem in the center of the inhabited world—and there must have been a good many more of these maps that have not survived.

I don't want to overstate the case. Not every medieval Christian accepted without question the centrality of Jerusalem. Yet at a certain moment in time, on a certain group of maps, this geographical convention captured a widespread belief about the world. Some scholars suggest that

that moment was tied to the Crusades, or, more specifically, to their failure. A world centered on Jerusalem became a symbol of hope after the city was lost to the Muslims in 1244.

Yet Jerusalem is more than a reflection of worldly affairs. On medieval maps, its geographical placement is nearly always intertwined with a bigger story: the death and resurrection of Jesus Christ. Most T-O maps that center on Jerusalem picture the saving work that Jesus did there. Some show Jerusalem by way of a church or basilica. Others depict one or three crosses. The tiny Psalter Map, which we will examine in more detail in chapter 7, shows Jerusalem as a red dot in the center of the world's circle—bull's-eye! (See fig. 3.)

Two maps of the medieval era focus on Jerusalem in a particularly arresting way. The Hereford Map, as we saw, centers on the crucifixion rising from the city of Jerusalem (see fig. 5). At the top of the cross hangs the titulus mentioned in the Gospel of John: "Jesus of Nazareth, King of the Jews." Ironically, this small picture, arguably the most important scene on the map, can be difficult to make out today. The Hereford Map has been through a lot in its seven hundred years, and some parts of it are severely degraded. Yet the ghost of Jesus can still be seen, rising up from the center to bring salvation to a world in need.

The Ebstorf Map, made around the same time as the Hereford Map, shows the glorious conclusion to the story—the resurrection. In Jerusalem, Jesus rises from the grave, while two soldiers slump below. Jesus holds a flag of victory in his hand (fig. 7).

The Hereford and Ebstorf Maps are closely related; they share the same vision of the world and many of the same geographical sites. I find it fascinating that one map centers on the crucifixion and the other on the resurrection. They picture the city of Jerusalem in different but complementary ways, bringing to the fore two defining moments in the saving work of Jesus Christ. In fact, it almost seems as though these maps are in dialogue with one another. Looking at them together, we are led to contemplate Jesus' sacrifice for the world and his victory over it.

These maps invite their viewers to reflect on what Jesus did at the center of the world. They make the argument that what he did was central to it. We see this in the specific way that Jerusalem is represented on the Hereford Map. Circular in shape, Jerusalem boasts crenellated walls encircling four towers and four gates. While other cities on the map are shown more or less at eye level, as if we were standing in front of them, we get a bird's-eye view

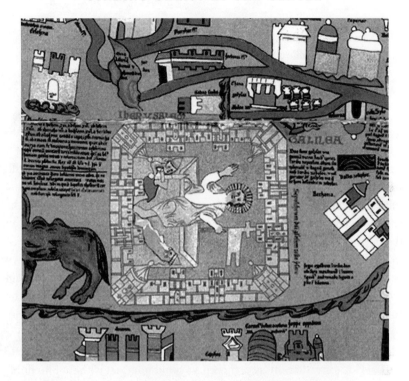

**FIGURE 7. Jerusalem with the resurrection inside the city walls.
Detail from the Ebstorf Map.**

of Jerusalem. For this reason, Jerusalem doesn't look particularly natural-istic. It is schematic, almost like a diagram. In fact, historian Evelyn Edson observes that the city's crenellated walls look "rather like a cog-wheel, the gear on which the whole universe turns."[1]

I find Edson's description of Jerusalem very apt. In fact, I cannot look at the Hereford Map without imaging the world spinning around the small but powerful gear of Jerusalem! But I would take Edson's statement one step further. If Jerusalem is the gear of the universe, the crucifixion is the lever that makes it go. The earth spins because of what happened in this small but world-altering city. It spins because of Jesus. When I see his cross at the center of the world, I am reminded of Paul's letter to the Colossians. Fol-lowing his greeting and prayer for the Colossian church, Paul opens with a beautiful hymn about Jesus, in which he proclaims,

---

1. Edson, *Mapping Time and Space*, 140.

> The Son is the image of the invisible God, the firstborn over all
> creation. For in him all things were created: things in heaven and
> on earth, visible and invisible, whether thrones or powers or rulers
> or authorities; all things have been created through him and for
> him. He is before all things, and in him all things hold together.
> (Col 1:15–17)

The Hereford Map gives us this picture: a world held together by Jesus Christ.

This christological way of seeing the world pervades medieval thought. It finds expression not only in maps but also in texts, ranging from the loftiest theological treatises to the most matter-of-fact discussions of the Christian life. Around the time the Hereford Map was made, a Franciscan theologian named John Duns Scotus reflected on the place of Jesus Christ in God's plan for the world. The doctrine he crafted, which today is known as the absolute primacy of Christ, states that Jesus was part of God's plan from the beginning of time—even before mankind sinned. The son is the fullest expression of the creator's love. He has always been part of the world.

I don't know that Scotus's theory had any connection to the Hereford Map, but it reminds me very strongly of it. On the map, Jesus is an intimate part of God's creation. Indeed, the world could not exist without him holding it together at the center. Looking at the map, I have no trouble believing, with Scotus, that Jesus was part of the picture from the very beginning.

A few years later, a travel writer known as Sir John Mandeville wrote a guide to the city of Jerusalem. This popular guide existed in hundreds of manuscript copies and helped shape how medieval people saw their world. It brings christological theology down to earth. In his guide, Sir John lists some of the travel routes from England to Jerusalem, but he opens with the same geo-historical mix that we see on T-O maps of the era:

> For he that will publish anything to make it openly known, he will
> make it to be cried and pronounced in the middle place of a town;
> so that the thing that is proclaimed and pronounced, may evenly
> stretch to all parts: right so, he that was former of all the world,
> would suffer for us at Jerusalem, that is the midst of the world;
> to that end and intent, that his passion and his death, that was
> published there, might be known evenly to all parts of the world.[2]

In this passage, we get an image of Jerusalem in the center of the world with "parts" all around it. It is like looking at a map. While the Hereford Map

2. Mandeville, *Travels*, 4.

pictures Jerusalem as a gear, Sir John describes a town crier who stands in the center of the city and, from this advantageous point, proclaims the good news of Jesus Christ for all to hear. Sir John makes clear the first principle of medieval geography: in centering on Jerusalem, the world centered on Jesus.

Sir John's prologue also contains a puzzle, rather like the puzzle of the chicken and the egg. Did Jesus suffer in Jerusalem because this city lies at the center of the world, or does Jerusalem lie at the center because Christ suffered there? Sir John appears to put geography first; yet his evocative description of the Gospel calling out to all parts of the world emphasizes faith. His reasoning is circular, like medieval maps themselves. He describes a world in which physical geography *is* spiritual geography.

Now we can return to our question and give it a better answer. Did medieval mapmakers really believe that Jerusalem lay at the center of the world? Yes. They believed it because they believed in the saving power of Jesus Christ, who brings good news to the world.

From View of the World to Worldview

With its vision of the cross rising from the city of Jerusalem, the Hereford Map offers more than a view of the world. It pictures a worldview. Although a philosophical concept, worldview is as real as geography. It describes the way we see and interpret the world around us. It encompasses our most cherished beliefs and the stories that give meaning to our lives. Everyone has a worldview, although not everyone thinks consciously about it. We all carry around beliefs and assumptions that shape the way we live. Have you given thought to some of yours?

Maps frequently point to worldviews. We sometimes think that maps are neutral, but this is a myth. Maps exist, writes Simon Garfield, to "relate and realign our history. They reflect our best and worst attributes—discovery and curiosity, conflict and destruction—and they chart our transitions of power. Even as individuals, we seem to have a need to plot a path and track our progress, to imagine possibilities of exploration and escape."[3] In other words, maps show what their users want and need to believe about the world. They allow us to daydream, to plot and scheme, to envision our future. They help us take journeys, both real and imagined. Maps are belief systems in miniature.

3. Garfield, *On the Map*, 18.

Maps with centers make their belief systems especially obvious. We have only to look at that one point—the bull's-eye in the middle—to discover what the people who made and used such a map hold most valuable. The Hereford Map is a prime example. This map shows thousands of valued sites in the medieval world. In the words of Evelyn Edson, it weaves "history, geography, botany, zoology, ethnology, and theology into one harmonious and dazzling whole."[4] The map contains so much information that it requires a bit of time to take it all in. Our eyes rove from exotic animals in the south to bustling commercial centers in the north to pilgrimage sites in the west to marvels of nature in the east. Yet the map reserves the center of the world for the sacred city of Jerusalem. Of all its dazzling sites, only the place of Jesus' death and resurrection occupies the true center.

The centrality of Jerusalem helps us negotiate some of the map's potentially troubling aspects. Modern viewers sometimes complain that the Hereford Map and its companions are Eurocentric. Unquestionably, these maps show the world from a Western perspective. The continent of Europe boasts more detail than any other part of the world; lesser-known regions and peoples are relegated to the edges of the earth. Medieval mapmakers made no effort to be politically correct. They portrayed *their* world and what they believed about it.

In an important way, however, medieval maps are not Eurocentric at all, since they reserve the center—the literal center—of the world for Jesus Christ. Europe is merely one continent that revolves around Jerusalem. For all its Westernism, the Hereford Map presents us with a truly Christ-centered worldview. The stories told about this world and the beliefs that keep it spinning all point to the man in the middle.

In centering on a sacred site, the Hereford Map follows a long tradition. Maps in the ancient world often privileged a significant spiritual locale. Mesopotamian maps centered on Babylon. Islamic maps centered on Mecca. And ancient Greek maps frequently centered on Delphi, the site of Apollo's oracle. Many scholars believe that medieval mapmakers took their basic geography at least partly from the ancient Greeks. They did not take the Greek center, however. They couldn't, for this was not the way they saw the world. Cartography followed conviction.

We encounter maps with centers in our world, too. On the world maps I saw growing up, North America always occupied the central position. So that the North American continent could have this pride of place, the great

4. Edson, *World Map*, 11.

Eurasian landmass was split in two, its left and right halves relegated to the edges of the map. This way of seeing the world—as divided, with "us" at the center and "them" everywhere else—seemed completely natural to me and to generations of schoolchildren in the United States. In many ways, it still does. Have you noticed that when you use Google Maps or program your GPS unit, you always see the world in relation to your own position? These satellite-based maps order geography around *us*. "We each stand, individually, at the center of our own map worlds," asserts Garfield.[5]

Some maps exaggerate our centrality to pointed effect. My city boasts a beautiful mural, titled *Welcome to the World*, on the side of a downtown building. The mural depicts a map with a curved surface like a globe. My own hometown dominates the globe and includes a portrait of some of its prominent buildings. The town then falls away into a cursory view of the rest of the country and the world (fig. 8). Note, for example, the pyramids of Egypt on the far right of the mural.

FIGURE 8. Justin Vining, *Welcome to the World*, 2010

These kinds of maps exploded in popularity after the appearance of Saul Steinberg's 1976 *New Yorker* cover drawing, *View of the World from 9th Avenue*, which shows a detailed view of Manhattan at the forefront of an abbreviated world. Does your hometown have a similar map?

My town's mural is painted opposite the salon that cuts my hair. As I sit for an unhurried hour or two, soaking up my stylist's undivided attention, I

5. Garfield, *On the Map*, 19.

like to look out the window at the mural and think about its meaning. Such maps, I believe, reveal our desire to dominate, to be "on top" of the world. Usually we keep this desire quiet. We talk about being a global village, but most of us don't mind hearing that the world is all about us (this is an especially appropriate message to receive on a visit to the hair salon!). We nurture the belief that we can be our own center.

As these examples show, the worldview pictured in the Hereford Map is not the only one on offer. We don't have to look far to find other belief systems, some of them quite appealing. If we are Christians, however, the Hereford Map's worldview really is the only viable one. It's the only game in town. This map, in which all things revolve around the cross, defines what we believe about Jesus Christ as revealed in the Bible. Throughout Scripture, everything points to Jesus. The Old Testament looks forward to him. The Gospels concern him. And the rest of the New Testament carries the good news forward to all times and places. Jesus is the center of God's revelation to the world.

Sir John Mandeville said that the Holy Land, specifically the city of Jerusalem, gives men "great solace and comfort." This is a good way to think about the medieval worldview. It is our comfort. Through it we affirm our belief in Jesus Christ and receive assurance that he is in control. He is holding our world together so that we don't have to.

A Medieval Merchant Finds His Center

The Hereford Map gives us a chance to see the Christ-centered worldview "in action." The map is not just a belief system, after all. It represents the world in which medieval people lived. With a little imagination, we can see how the map might have influenced Christians to interpret their experiences as they made their way through this world. In the fourteenth century, the map's viewers were likely to be pilgrims who journeyed to Hereford Cathedral, where the map was housed. These pilgrims came from different walks of life. Some were nobles, but most seem to have been craftsmen, peasants, and wanderers such as minstrels and merchants. According to cathedral records, some pilgrims made the trek to Hereford every year.

Let us imagine an English merchant, a man who lived in the Cotswolds and worked in the all-important wool trade. Let us say that one fine spring day, he traveled with a group of pilgrims to Hereford. Entering the cathedral and walking up its nave, he caught sight of the map—a giant, four-foot image of the world that was like nothing he'd ever seen (fig. 9).[6]

FIGURE 9. Digital reconstruction showing the Hereford Map as it might have been situated in Hereford Cathedral in the early fourteenth century. The tomb of Saint Thomas Cantilupe is located to the left of the map.

On this map, the merchant saw sites of interest in his world, most of them located on the continent of Europe. Current events might have drawn his eye. The map, for example, illustrates King Edward I's new castle at Caernarfon, on which construction had begun in 1283. The merchant had heard others grumble about the extravagance of the king's new project,

6. Terkla, "Original Placement," proposes that the map was located in the north transept of the cathedral, next to the shrine of Saint Thomas Cantilupe, as seen in figure 9.

but he admired the industry that went into it. (He didn't admire the king's new taxes, however.)

Of course the merchant noted that the map plots several cities along the trade routes by which English wool was carried through France to Italy. He sighed as he remembered that he himself would be back on the road as soon as he completed this pilgrimage. He had flocks to inspect, prices to haggle over, and, of course, tax collectors to dodge.

Someone beside him nudged him and pointed to a different area of the map. There, along the River Wye, was the city of Hereford itself (fig. 10).

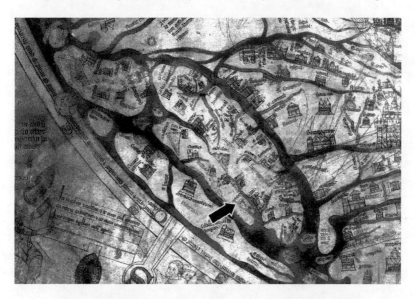

FIGURE 10. The black arrow points to the city of Hereford on the River Wye. Detail from the Hereford Map. This part of the map has been degraded from repeated touching by medieval pilgrims.

The merchant reached over and touched it, remembering why he had made the journey to the cathedral. Most of his fellow pilgrims had come to Hereford to profit from the healing power of the remains of Saint Thomas Cantilupe. A group of people thronged around the saint's shrine now, touching it and leaving small gifts. The merchant had just knelt there himself and prayed fervently for healing from the pains in his back that had afflicted him for the past several months. They made travel difficult, and travel was his life.

As he stood before the map, the merchant therefore saw fragments of his work, his home, and his suffering and need. The various parts of his life were plotted on this vast image of the world. He might also have noted more distant sites. Gazing at the continent of Asia, the merchant perhaps thought of acquaintances that had been fortunate enough to take a pilgrimage to the Holy Land. He himself would probably never be able to make this holy journey, tied as he was to the ebb and flow of the wool trade.

Of course, pilgrims went to the Holy Land primarily to see the place where Jesus had died and rose again. The merchant traveled there now with his eyes. Looking at the map, he fastened his gaze on the crucifixion rising up in the midst of the earth. People jostled him, wanting him to move on, yet he lingered a moment longer. The sight of Jerusalem gave him comfort. It reminded him that none of his problems or responsibilities were too big for Jesus. And none were big enough to take over his world. A sense of relief flooded him. His faith was renewed. He had found, once again, his center.

The Challenge for Our World

We, too, can find our center in Christ. Like our merchant pilgrim, we can see in the Hereford Map a picture of our faith, our world, and be reassured that Jesus is holding it together. If you are like me, you need this assurance. The world is a big and uncertain place. Sometimes, it is a dangerous place, full of hardship, sin (our own and others'), and unknowns. Yet whatever happens, we know that our world will not come crashing down on our heads. It cannot, for Jesus centers it, as he has from the beginning of time. He steadies the world, making it a safe place to travel. We can put our faith in him.

Yet as we go along, we find it easy to lose sight of our center. We are born wanderers. Our soul, as the seventeenth-century mystic Madame Guyon puts it, has acquired the habit of "being always abroad."[7] We have a savior who loves us and lays claim to us. As our center, he draws us to him. Life, however, seems determined to pull us away. Other responsibilities and commitments, sometimes even other beliefs, compete for our attention. Before we know it, we have chased after them and ended up somewhere we never intended to be—somewhere far from the center of our world.

In 2012, Barna Group conducted a study of Christian women today. The results are revealing. When asked to name their highest priority in life,

7. Guyon, *Short and Very Easy Method of Prayer*, 235.

53 percent of Christian women polled chose family. They find their identity in their role as a parent. Jesus came in at a distant second; 16 percent polled reported their faith as their top priority.[8]

Sometimes I think about the answer I would give to this question. Like the women in the Barna study, I am a follower of Jesus, one who finds the center of the universe utterly compelling. Yet my faith is imperfect. My own tendency, I well know, is to make my work my highest priority. I place great store in the satisfaction I take in writing and speaking—and the occasional success I find in them. It's a dangerous way to live, because every small success tempts me to think that if I work hard enough, I can rely on myself. I come to believe that I'll be able to hold my world together.

The Barna Group study isn't about other people, as much as I would like it to be. It's about me. It's about all of us who struggle to live out our faith on a daily basis. The fact is, it's hard to put our money where our mouth is. We may define ourselves as Christians yet be tempted to put something (or someone) else at the center of our world. We love Jesus and want to put our trust in him, but in our day-to-day life, other beliefs creep in.

This is why the Hereford Map can be of such value in our walk of faith. With the help of the map, we can pause in our journey and get back on track. We can get back to the basics. The map reminds us that Jesus—and only Jesus—holds our world together. We may cherish our family and want to raise our children well. We may delight in putting to use the gifts God has given us in work and ministry. All these things have a good and right place in our world. That place, however, is not the center. The center belongs to Jesus Christ, and him crucified. Only Jesus can save us.

The map, in other words, encourages us to adopt a truly Christ-centered worldview. It points us to a way of life consistent with what the Bible claims about Jesus. As I go through life, I try to live out this world-view. I try to live *in* it. Following the example of our merchant pilgrim, I like to imagine my world as a circle, like the medieval world. I picture the parts of my life, or the different roles I play—mother, writer, churchgoer—scattered throughout the circle. The paths I take go every which way. Yet at the center of them all, I see Jesus.

This is an exercise I try to do frequently. It is most often a mental exercise, although sometimes I take out a piece of paper and draw a map of my world. It helps me as I strive to order my life around Jesus. My life is full—full of risk and responsibilities, problems and pleasures. Yet amidst

8. Barna Group, "What Women Want."

the busyness, I know what sustains me: not institutions that fail or people who, being people, inevitably let me down. And certainly not myself. I don't have to reach deep down inside for something that isn't there. Instead, I reach for Jesus.

And I smile. I feel the satisfaction of a medieval mapmaker who has anchored his compass in the middle of the earth. My circle has a center. All is right with the world.

Reflections and Practices

- What answer would you give to the Barna Group survey? What is the highest priority in your life?

- Look at the city of Jerusalem at the center of the Hereford Map. As you do, meditate on Paul's description of Jesus' place in the world: "For in him all things were created: things in heaven and on earth, visible and invisible, whether thrones or powers or rulers or authorities; all things have been created through him and for him. He is before all things, and in him all things hold together" (Col 1:16–17).

- Try the exercise mentioned at the end of this chapter. Draw the circular outline of a medieval map divided into the three continents of the world. Write or sketch in the parts of your life in the different geographical areas of the world. Now place the city of Jerusalem at the center of the map. See, through this exercise, how Jesus plants himself in the middle of your world!

- Pray that Jesus would give you the faith to believe in him, and him alone, as your savior. Sometimes, I like to pray the simple words of the father whose son Jesus cured of an impure spirit: "I do believe; help me overcome my unbelief!" (Mark 9:24)

3

Finding Christ in History

If I asked you to write your history, where would you begin? With your parents? With the crossing of your ancestors on the Mayflower? Would you begin as far back as you could trace your family name? I know someone who has traced her family to John of Gaunt, Duke of Lancaster and a son of King Edward III! I find that pretty impressive.

I think that medieval historians would have, too. Like today's genealogists, they wanted to find their place in history, and they were experts at going back in time. The further back, the better. They didn't have the programs and apps that we do. But they had something just as good—maps. Maps were closely linked to history in the Middle Ages. Sometimes, maps were added to chronicles. Philip III, king of France, owned a royal history that included a small world map as one of its illustrations.

Some medieval maps boasted so many historical details that they stood on their own as a form of "visual chronicle." The Hereford Map is a good example. On this map, a vast and beautiful history unfurls. As we travel the map, the chapters in this history come into focus. They tell the story of God moving through time to fulfill his promises to the world.

When medieval Christians wanted to find their place in the world, they told this story. They wrote it, illustrated it, and mapped it. The history of the world played a role in their spiritual life. Through the Hereford Map, these Christians teach us to become historians, too. I'm not talking about a history that is dead and gone or one whose only value lies in teaching us lessons from a distant past. The map tells a living history. It is the history, the ongoing story, of God, the world, and us.

Using the Hereford Map, we will learn, in this chapter, to be historians of our faith. Even if you've never researched your ancestry or your college career never included a front-row seat in History 101, the map's story is for you. It is for every Christian, because it narrates God's plan of salvation from the world's beginning to its end. We all have a stake in this story. We all need to claim it. In fact, thinking historically leads to spiritual growth, to the kind of self-assurance that God wants us to have. We will find, as we follow the history of the world from chapter to chapter on the Hereford Map, that our knowledge of God is deepened and our faith strengthened. We may even discover that our sense of significance has grown as big as the earth itself.

History 101—Creation

How do we learn to think historically? We begin at the beginning. The Hereford Map takes us there. At the top of the map, we see the garden of Eden, which was often called Earthly Paradise in the Middle Ages. As the name implies, it's a bit of heaven brought to earth. A walled garden whose circular shape echoes that of the planet, Earthly Paradise evokes the moment when God set the world spinning in the heavens. It affords us a glimpse of God's creativity—the creation itself (fig. 11).

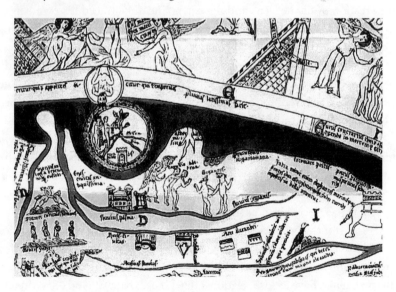

FIGURE 11. Earthly Paradise, the circular garden at the top of the map. Detail from the Hereford Map. This part of the map is so degraded that its details are best viewed in facsimile, as in this illustration.

It can be difficult to get used to seeing Earthly Paradise on a map. Yet medieval theologians believed that it existed on earth. In the words of Saint Bede, writing in the eighth century,

> Let us have no doubt that the paradise in which the first human being was placed is to be understood as a real place, even if we also regard it as a figure of the present Church or of our future fatherland. The text [the book of Genesis] speaks of a place of delights, shaded by fruit trees, and of a broad dwelling place, from which sprang a great river.[1]

This river, mentioned in Genesis, divided and became four rivers that flowed from the garden to water the earth. They are visible in the Hereford Map's Eden, providing a link between the world and its moment of creation.

In the Middle Ages, serious historians began the search for their place in the world with the creation. They used this event to measure time and even to encode personal histories. In the fifteenth century, Philip the Good, third Valois duke of Burgundy, owned a chronicle that included the foundation story of one of his most important territories. This chronicle helped Philip use the past to better plan his future. But the chronicle delved far deeper into the past than the birth of his territories. How did it begin? With the creation of the heavens and the earth. The duke traced his own beginnings to that first, distant beginning, shrouded in mystery yet part of living history.

Philip the Good may have been guided more by ambition than by faith, but he points us toward a biblical interpretation of the past. The creation, as he clearly believed, forms part of every Christian's history. We are part of an unbroken chain of events that began in Eden or perhaps even earlier. In his letter to the Ephesians, the Apostle Paul asserts that God "chose us in him before the creation of the world to be holy and blameless in his sight. In love he predestined us for adoption to sonship through Jesus Christ, in accordance with his pleasure and will—to the praise of his glorious grace, which he has freely given us in the One he loves" (Eph 1:4–6).

The storyteller Steven James reflects on what these verses mean for our place in history. Speaking of God, he writes, "While darkness swirled around him, he dreamt about us and he loved us. His unchanging plan has always been to have a close relationship with us. That was God's first dream, and it gave him great pleasure. Then he shaped the world backward through

---

1. Quoted in Delumeau, *History of Paradise*, 19.

time so that we would arrive at just the right moment in just the right place on just the right planet as part of a divine, intergalactic dream-come-true."[2]

When I read to my children from their Bible, I like telling them that they, as much as the flora and fauna of Genesis 1, as much as Adam and Eve themselves, belong to the story of creation. It blows their minds, as well it should. It is quite audacious to date our story from the moment God made the world. Yet it is also biblical—and very medieval, as we can see from history lovers like Philip the Good and from the Hereford Map itself. When we look at the top of the map, we are gazing upon our own origins. Our history begins here—in the beginning.

History 101—Sin

In the beginning, we find another early chapter of our history—sin. In the walled garden at the top of the Hereford Map, we get a glimpse of our first parents (see fig. 11). Standing before the tree of knowledge, Adam and Eve take the forbidden fruit, and the journey of humanity begins. The sequel to the story plays out below, where a sword-brandishing angel drives the first parents from the garden.

Adam and Eve leave the garden in grief. Eve places her hand on Adam's shoulder, as if she were blind, and Adam wrings his hands in front of his stooped body. He looks back at the garden he has just left. It is no wonder they react so dramatically. Adam and Eve are no longer denizens of paradise. They have to work for a living, and they become acquainted with shame, fear, and pain. They experience the consequences of sin.

The birth of sin into the world is shown on the map in another, even more dramatic, way—and in another part of the world. If we travel from the tip of Asia to the continent of Africa, we come face to face with a series of strange creatures inhabiting the southern coastline of the world. They are monsters. The technical term is "monstrous races," groups of part-human, part-animal creatures said, in the Middle Ages, to live at the edge of civilization. Sir John Mandeville, who wrote a popular travel guide in the fourteenth century, defines a monster as "a thing deformed against kind both of man or of beast or of anything else."[3] Not quite human, not quite animal, the monstrous races are liminal creatures and thus to be feared—or at least treated with a healthy respect.

2. James, *Story*, 20.
3. Mandeville, *Travels*, 32.

The Hereford Map pictures twenty monstrous creatures along its southern edge. Each one is distinguished by unique physical attributes and social behaviors that set it apart from more "civilized" areas of the world. Let's take a closer look at some of these unusual creatures.

FIGURE 12. Monsters along the edge of Africa. Detail from the Hereford Map.

Beginning at the top of figure 12, we first meet a Sciopod, a popular medieval monster with a single leg. When the sun beat down, Sciopods lay on their backs and extended their giant foot over their body for shade. Across the Nile from the Sciopod are the Amyctyrae, one of whom shades himself with his giant lip, which he pulls up over his face. Below the Sciopod is a Straw-Drinker, who has no nose or mouth but takes in nourishment by inserting a straw into an orifice on his face. The final monster in this illustration is a representative of the Androgini, who have characteristics of both sexes; they can inseminate themselves without benefit of a mate.

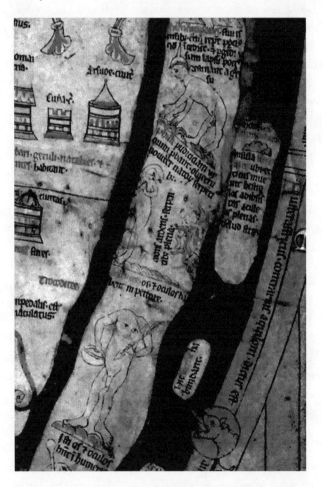

FIGURE 13. More monsters along the edge of Africa. Detail from the Hereford Map.

The monstrous races continue in figure 13. Here we see, at the top of the image, a Himantopode, who glides on all fours on long, straplike feet. Below are the Psylli, who expose newborns to serpents to test their mothers' chastity. At the bottom of the image we meet the Blemmyae, headless people with faces in their chests.

The Hereford Map presents but a sampling of medieval monsters. In bestiaries, travel guides, and maps, the Middle Ages catalogued more than eighty monstrous races. In part, the oddities assigned to these creatures stemmed from fear of the unknown. The continent of Africa was relatively unexplored in the Middle Ages. Stories about this part of the world proliferated, and few of them were based on firsthand knowledge. Lore and legend reigned. In fact, the medieval world inherited most of its monsters from the classical era, in which they populated the texts of such esteemed writers as Pliny the Elder. The physical and cultural attributes of the monstrous races were passed down from writer to writer and map to map. Fear was passed down, too.

The monstrous races also came to be part of distinctly medieval discussions in the fields of theology and history. Despite and even because of their unusual features, the monsters were thought to play a role in the grand drama of salvation. This is how we will examine them here—as an early chapter in the ongoing story of God's creation. The monsters' starring role in sacred history heightened their disturbing nature, giving medieval Christians one more reason to fear everyone and everything on the edge of the world.

The monsters' story begins in the book of Genesis, some six chapters after Adam and Eve were driven from Earthly Paradise. It's a story of sin shaping the world—in this case, shaping it quite literally. We learned in chapter 2 that medieval mapmakers divided the world into three continents. The explanation for this division comes from the story of Noah and the flood. Genesis 10 tells us that, after the flood, Noah's three sons—Shem, Ham, and Japheth—founded the people groups from which all humanity descended. The text lists their descendants in genealogical tables, occasionally singling out prominent ancestors for extra comment, and concludes, "From these the nations spread out over the earth after the flood" (Gen 10:32).

Although the Bible does not precisely define the geographical regions that Noah's sons inherited, medieval historians came to identify each son with one of the three inhabited continents of the world. According to this theory, Shem inherited Asia, Ham inherited Africa, and Japheth inherited Europe. On some T-O maps, the name of each son appears next to the name of the continent he inherited, just to make the relationship clear to viewers. A small map illustrating a fifteenth-century historical text pictures the sons of Noah, making history and geography come alive (fig. 14). Noah's ark can be seen above Shem on the continent of Asia, reminding us of the biblical origins of this genealogical story.

Each of Noah's sons takes his place in the story of humanity. But, as so often happens, history remembers the siblings quite differently. For medieval historians, the most important son was Shem, from whom Jesus himself descended. Ham, however, caused some consternation. According to Saint Jerome, Ham inherited Africa because his name means "hot."[4] But, as we read in Genesis, Ham was also a bit hotheaded. After the flood, Noah

FIGURE 14. T-O map showing the sons of Noah, ca. 1455

4. Friedman, *Monstrous Races*, 101.

got drunk on wine and lay uncovered in his tent. Shem and Japheth looked away from Noah, but Ham, who is twice called the father of Canaan (vv. 18 and 22), did not. When Noah awoke, he said, "Cursed be Canaan! The lowest of slaves will he be to his brothers" (Gen 9:25).

Ham's family was cursed because Ham mocked Noah—and, according to some apocryphal sources, because he had relations with his wife on the ark despite Noah's call for sexual abstinence. Because of his sin, medieval theologians and historians said, Ham went on to father a nation of monsters that outwardly expressed the corruption of their souls. The monstrous races were born.

Some medieval texts push the origins of the monstrous races further back in time—to Cain, son of Adam and Eve and the world's first murderer. The Hereford Map contains an inscription on the northeastern rim of Asia that speaks of "exceedingly savage people who eat human flesh and drink blood, the accursed sons of Cain." As we will see in a later chapter, it was believed that Alexander the Great walled up these "sons of Cain" so that they would not bring the world to an untimely end. Cain was also thought by some historians to have fathered the monstrous races on the edge of Africa. Cain, like Ham, was cursed. He was also marked physically by God, a fact that made it easy to believe that his sons—the monstrous races—suffered gross deformities.

Of these progenitors, Ham is the more troubling because of his association with the continent of Africa. Over the centuries, Ham's curse came to be cited in support of racist ideas, such as the belief that the peoples of Africa deserved to be enslaved to other nations. These beliefs, and the actions of those who held them, are truly monstrous. They add to the stack of sins for which many nations and persons still owe repentance today.

Medieval writers and artists were themselves capable of expressing prejudice, especially toward unfamiliar places and peoples. As we saw, the monstrous races represented, in part, fear of the "other." They were the great unknowns of the great big world. Yet one of the texts that most influenced medieval thinking, Saint Augustine's *City of God*, provides a more gracious view of the monstrous races. Augustine begins by debating the existence of these creatures. He finds it reasonable to believe that they are real and concludes that they must display a common human nature:

> But whoever is anywhere born a man, that is, a rational, mortal animal, no matter what unusual appearance he presents in colour, movement, sound, nor how peculiar he is in some power, part, or

quality of his nature, no Christian can doubt that he springs from that one protoplast [i.e., Adam].[5]

Augustine appeals to the shared origins of humankind; he points out the thread that connects all people in the midst of their differences. The Hereford Map does so, too. The map links the monstrous races to Adam and especially to his descendants, Cain and Ham. It shows that the mysterious creatures on the edge of the earth were not just "other" to the Western world. They also formed a chapter in the history of the entire world. It's not a particularly glorious chapter; its plot points center on willful disobedience and fallen humanity. This troubling chapter, like sin itself, affects the world over. We are all descendants of Adam.

History 101—Salvation

The cure for monsters—the very remedy for sin—is found in the middle of the world. When we travel from the edge of the Hereford Map to the city at its center, we find the cross of Christ. In chapter 2, we examined the idea that Christ holds the world together. Now we see that he also holds the key to time. The crucifixion shapes history. "From Adam on to the Kingdom of God we can trace in the Bible the thread of one single movement which finds its center in the death and the resurrection of Christ," writes historian Theo Preiss.[6] We see this movement on the Hereford Map, in which, at the precise center of the world, Jesus directs the course of history. At the center, Jesus defeated the monsters of sin and death. At the center, he gives the world hope and a future.

The Hereford Map illustrates a fair number of *anno domini* events, such as the flowering of Christianity, the rise of the Roman Empire, and the dominance of the medieval West. The latter is shown by sites like Paris, Rome, and, of course, Hereford itself (fig. 15).

5. Augustine, *City of God*, 16.8 (Dods, 531).
6. Preiss, "Christian Philosophy of History," 162.

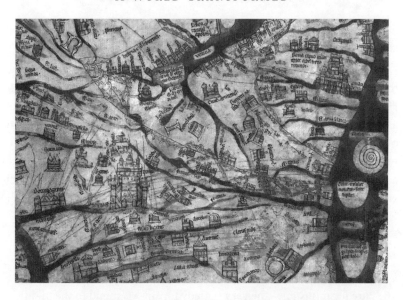

FIGURE 15. The bustling continent of Europe. Note the large cities of Paris, slightly off-center, and Rome, on the far right near the top. Detail from the Hereford Map.

We have evidence that medieval viewers of the map delighted in seeing their little corner of the world: they touched the city of Hereford so much that they nearly wore this part of the map away (see fig. 10 in chapter 2). Part of their delight must have come in discovering that they had a place in the map's story of salvation.

We can make the same discovery. When visitors come to Hereford Cathedral today, they, too, touch the map, which is protected by a glass covering. They touch the city of Hereford, and some people touch other places, perhaps their hometowns or cities they have visited on the continent of Europe. The fingerprints they leave "tell exactly the same story they did when the map was new," says Dominic Harbour, commercial director at the cathedral.[7] They tell the story of people searching for their place in the world. No less than the map's original viewers, present-day pilgrims are witness to an age that is part of God's grand design, to a time and a place that, like all times and places in history, finds its center in the saving work of Jesus Christ.

History comes to a close at the top of the map, where, above Earthly Paradise, Jesus judges the living and the dead. To his right are the saved,

7. Quoted in Garfield, *On the Map*, 56. Garfield reports on the fingerprints left by tourists to the cathedral.

who rise from their graves and follow angels to the gate of heaven, and to his left are the damned, roped and dragged to the jaws of hell. Earthly life is now over, and eternity begins, or is revealed, baser realities no longer veiling it from our view. Jesus himself sits on a throne, his nail-pierced hands spread wide (fig. 16). He is the Christ of Revelation, who proclaims, "Yes, I am coming soon."

And God's people respond, "Amen. Come, Lord Jesus" (Rev 22:20).

FIGURE 16. The Last Judgment. Detail from the Hereford Map. This illustration comes from a nineteenth-century facsimile of the map.

From "In the Beginning" to "Amen"

Now that we have reached the end of time, we can step back and see where the Hereford Map has taken us. It is quite a journey. We have traveled to the garden of Eden, the edge of Africa, medieval Jerusalem, and the gates of heaven. These places do not seem terribly familiar, geographically speaking. They are exotic, almost otherworldly. But together, they form chapters in a story that is well known to us. They provide the framework for the Bible's message of salvation. In the words of Robert Webber,

> The framework of that message is that God created the world; that the world fell away from God in the disobedience of the first Adam; that God rescued the world through Jesus Christ, the second Adam; and that at the end of history God will complete the rescue operation in the establishment of the new heavens and the new earth.[8]

The Bible tells the story of creation, sin, and salvation, the great drama that stretches from "In the beginning" to "Amen." It is the story of God saving the world.

As we move from site to site on the Hereford Map, we visit the events that make up this story. Each event is rich, inviting us to pause, dig deep, and reflect. In chapter 2, for example, we spent some time reflecting on the crucifixion at the center of the map and what it means for our lives. It is my belief that we can't spend too much time meditating on Jesus' sacrifice for us. Yet the Hereford Map gives us a second way to look at this event. When we widen our focus, we see that the crucifixion forms the center of a vast history beginning with the creation and ending with the second coming. In a few glances, we can take in the whole story of salvation. We see God's big picture.

Both ways of seeing God's story have value. Most of us are probably used to taking in the story one chapter at a time. We dip into the Bible to read the stories or verses that seem most relevant to our situation. Perhaps we follow a schedule of readings or attend a study group that delves into one book of the Bible. This is certainly good. From time to time, however, we need to hear the whole story, from beginning to end. When we do, we get a glimpse of the mind of God, who holds time and eternity in his hands. What wonderful plans he has for our world! He is bringing everything to the glorious fulfillment that he foretold.

The grandeur of the Hereford Map reminds me of the night sky. When the weather is good and I can get away from the city, I like to look up at the stars. I try to piece together a few constellations. If I'm lucky, I'll see a couple of planets, too, piercing the sky with bright points of light. On nights like this, I never want to go in. I have front row seats to a slice of eternity.

The Hereford Map elicits a similar feeling of awe. When I look at this map, I realize that the same creator who set the planets spinning also set time in motion. And his timeline is still going on. From the first moments of history to the last, which we glimpse but dimly, the plans of God are

---

8. Webber, *Ancient-Future Faith*, 46.

spread before us on the map, as bright and piercing as the stars in the heavens. I can't help marveling at the grandeur of God's plans for creation—and my own place in it.

The Challenge for Our World

I will never forget the first time I caught a glimpse of God's plans for the world. I was a teenager, and it was Advent. On Christmas Eve, the church in which I grew up held a Festival of Nine Lessons and Carols, a type of service that originated in England in the early twentieth century. The lessons began with readings from the book of Genesis and proceeded through the Old Testament prophecies about Jesus before culminating in the familiar Christmas story from the Gospels. I loved sitting through this long service. The hour was late. The church was candlelit. The lessons brought us closer and closer to Jesus. All was anticipation.

Yet what thrilled me most, what I remember most, was the first lesson of the service. The reading took us to the garden of Eden, after the fall of humanity, when God reveals that Adam's seed will bruise the serpent's head: "And I will put enmity between you and the woman, and between your offspring and hers; he will crush your head, and you will strike his heel" (Gen 3:15).

Waiting for Jesus, I was suddenly transported to the beginning of time. Christmas was revealed for what it is: not an isolated feast but the center of a vast history that began in the mind of God and that will not end until the day of judgment. Driving home after the service, beneath a dome of glittery stars, I knew that Jesus was part of something incredibly big. And since I claimed Jesus, whose birth I was celebrating—or rather, since he claimed me—I was part of something big, too.

What a wonderful moment. My place in the world, my significance in the grand scheme of things, was presented to me like a gift from God. Since that night, I have tried to hold on to this certain knowledge of my significance. But it's difficult. The world seems bent on putting me in my place—a very small place. As we all do, I face rejection on a daily basis. I compare myself with other people and come up wanting. I feel misused and overlooked. Sometimes, at the end of a difficult day, it can seem that God himself has forgotten about me.

History tells me otherwise. And when I feel small, I need a big dose of it—a dose the size of the Hereford Map. God's people need to tell his story.

We need to rehearse it, revel in it, and get lost in its grandeur. When we do, we realize how wide—and at the same time how welcoming—God's story really is. Dorothy Bass reflects, "Amazingly, even though this story began before time itself and reaches beyond the end of time, it is a story that has room in its narrative for each individual who encounters it in the present day."[9] When we get lost in God's story, we find ourselves.

Bass suggests that we enter God's story by celebrating the church year, which, through its liturgical seasons, takes us through key points in the "life of God." I like the idea of paying attention to sacred history throughout the year, as I did at that Christmas Eve service long ago. This is one reason I go to church every Sunday, even when I don't feel like getting my family ready and out the door. I endure the drama of dressing two small girls, each with her own idea of what constitutes appropriate churchgoing attire, so that we can participate in an even bigger drama. We need to be reminded that we have a role in the story God is telling about the world.

I find another point of connection to God's story in the Hereford Map. Sitting down with a good reproduction of the map, I let history wash over me. My eyes roam over the map's sacred sites, from Eden to Africa to Jerusalem to the gates of heaven. If you try this exercise yourself, you will see that the map organizes these sites in a particular way. It lays out salvation like a diagram. The creation and the birth of sin take place at the edges of the world, as if to show their distance from human experience and understanding. Jesus lies at the center. Time ends, and eternity begins, at the top.

In between these pivotal sites in the history of salvation, there is a lot of room—all the room in the world. There is room for the medieval Christians who were the map's first users, and room for you and me. Room for our stories. Room for our mistakes. Room for our redemption. Room to recover our significance.

In fact, every follower of Christ finds herself on the map of salvation every day, in ordinary but breathtaking ways. Have you ever had a bad day? Have you ever let sin get the best of you and then knelt humbly to ask God's forgiveness? That's part of my day *every* day. It's also part of the grand design of God. When we sin and ask forgiveness, we are playing our role in the drama of salvation—the very drama illustrated on the Hereford Map. We journey from the monstrous races at the edge of the world to the cross at the center. We make the journey of God's saving grace.

9. Bass, *Receiving the Day*, 80–81.

Each time we turn to Jesus in our day, whether in desperation, worship, or repentance, we turn to the center of history. Point to the city of Jerusalem on the Hereford Map. That's where you stand (or kneel) every time you pray or praise God, every time you read the Bible or bear the fruit of the Spirit. Even our smallest acts of living faithfully inscribe us in God's story. They make us players in the drama of the Bible.

Let us learn, then, to embrace our place in God's plan. Let's learn to think big. No more false humility. No more wondering where we belong or whether we matter in the grand scheme of things. We do matter. And we belong on the map of salvation.

When we are convinced that we matter, we can do great things for God. We can make the move we've been hesitating to make or take the leap of faith God is asking us to take. We can put aside our fear and become, in all confidence, who we know God wants us to be. We may even make our mark in history, like some of the saints who have gone before us!

For now, it is enough to make our mark on the map. One step at a time, one day at a time, we take the Hereford Map's journey through history, a journey that is taking us all the way to eternity. One day, our steps will take us to the top of the map, where Jesus presides over the end of the world. We will stand before him and be received at the throne of grace. Until that time, we faithfully walk the route of redemption. We may be small, one little cog in the machinery of salvation, but our story helps keep the world spinning.

Reflections and Practices

- Go outside on a clear night and spend some time looking at the stars. Give praise that the God who set the heavens in motion is bringing our world to redemption.

- Using the image of the Hereford Map in figure 1, trace the Bible's story of salvation—from creation, at the top of the world, to sin, at the edge, to salvation, at the center, and to the final judgment, once again at the top.

- Meditate on Jeremiah 29:11 as you look at the Hereford Map's story of salvation: "'For I know the plans I have for you,' declares the LORD, 'plans to prosper you and not to harm you, plans to give you hope and a future.'" Rejoice that God has made you part of his plans for the world. You have a place in the great drama of salvation!

4

Finding Christ at the Edge

In the past few months, my older daughter has begun to comment on the not so great moments of my mothering career. "I don't like that voice," she says when I begin to get impatient. Or, "why are you making your mean face?"

These are sobering comments. They act as the reminder I need to slow down—to pause, take a deep breath, and take stock of what is going on. The truth is, I don't like "that voice" either. I know the one my daughter means. When I start to lose it, my voice gets an edge. My whole being feels on edge—the edge of motherhood, the edge of my patience, the edge of my faith. It is a dangerous place to be. I am standing on a precipice, and things can go either way: I can go over the edge, or I can return to being the person my daughter needs me to be.

These are the times when I most need to see Jesus in my world: the everyday moments in which I struggle to live out the day with a modicum of grace. We learned in chapter 3 that we have a place in God's grand plan of redemption for the world. We need to know that we are part of God's "big picture." Yet I also need God in the details. There is no moment so small or insignificant that I do not require his aid. In fact, these mundane moments, when I am caring for my children, doing chores, or banging out words so that I can meet my writing quota for the day, are precisely the ones that threaten to do me in. I need God to pull me back from the edge.

Yet these difficult times are often the very ones in which I feel God's absence. I do not really believe that God removes himself in my moments of need. Rather, I forget to look for him. When I am on edge, I tend to develop a severe case of myopia. I dwell on myself and my problems to the exclusion of everything else, and I easily lose sight of God.

In some of the arresting images on medieval maps, I have discovered landmarks to help me find my way back to God. The Hereford Map and its companion, the Ebstorf Map, give me a language to voice my frustration and to see Jesus in the darker areas of my life. From these maps, I learn the extent of God's care and compassion for the world and for every soul struggling through difficult moments in the journey of life.

The Hereford Map provides a particularly vivid metaphor for my feeling of being on edge. On this map, the edge is a geographical reality. Take a moment and trace the outline of the Hereford Map in figure 1. You have just found the edge—a line of demarcation, sharp as a blade, that circles the world, dividing land and water, known and unknown, civilization and the void. When you reach the edge of this map, you can go no farther. You have come to the end of all things.

Appearances to the contrary, the makers of this map didn't really think that the earth was a flat disk with a cookie-cutter edge. They knew that the earth was a sphere. It appears flat on the map partly because of the difficulty of portraying the world as a sphere and partly because a flat earth allowed mapmakers to organize reality in a certain way. It let them illustrate the earth as a kind of diagram, packed full of data. It also let them give the earth an edge—a danger zone that stood in opposition to everything that was good and familiar about the world.

In the edge, we find a symbol of the difficulties in our own world. First, we have to suspend our disbelief. The Hereford Map is colorful. It describes sights along the edge that may make us chuckle or shake our head with disbelief. "They put *this* on their maps?" Take these sights seriously, at least for now. See in them signs and landmarks for experiences you might have had or hard times you have gone through. If you do, you will find in the medieval edge a way to cry out to God—and, if you look closely, an opportunity to find his saving grace.

A World of Monsters

On the edge of the medieval world, monsters roamed. We met some of them in chapter 3, the creatures whose physical deformities were outward signs of the curse of Ham. The sons of Ham inhabited the continent of Africa on medieval maps. But we can define their geographical location even more precisely. If you take another look at the Hereford Map, you will see that the monstrous races have been relegated to the edge of the continent—the end of all things. To make sure they stay put, a narrow branch of the Nile River cuts them off from the interior of the world.

An equal number of monsters can be found on the edge of Asia, along the eastern rim of the world. On the Hereford Map, we meet, for example, a Sciopod, who uses his single giant foot to shade himself from the sun, and the Pygmies, who stand one cubit high (fig. 17).

FIGURE 17. A Sciopod shading his head. On the right, four Pygmies stand atop the mountains of India. Detail from the Hereford Map.

Below are pictured the Astomi (Apple-Smellers), who live on the scent of fruit. They take apples on trips and will die if they smell a bad odor (fig. 18). Whereas the monsters in medieval Africa stood for sin and moral depravity, the creatures in Asia represented the mystery of unknown and exotic lands. Asia was home to the Holy Land, so the monsters in this continent had a certain (if sometimes dangerous) appeal.

In very few cases are humans from the "civilized" world shown interacting with the monstrous creatures. In Africa, especially, these creatures inhabited a part of the world to which most Europeans did not dare to go. Yet the Hereford Map does allude to one very interesting story of human-monster interaction. Near the upper mouth of the Nile River, the map pictures the monasteries of Saint Anthony, an early desert saint. Anthony lived in Egypt, which was considered to be part of Asia on many maps of the medieval period. Just below the monasteries—and far bigger in size— roams a satyr, a creature with a human torso, a birdlike head, a tail, and cleft hooves (fig. 19).

FIGURE 18. Two Astomi (Apple-Smellers) harvesting and sniffing apples from a tree. Detail from the Hereford Map.

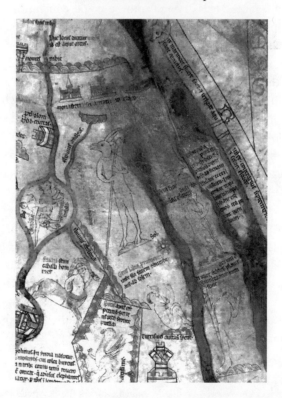

FIGURE 19. In the center of the image is the satyr that tempted Saint Anthony. The monasteries of Saint Anthony lie above the satyr. Detail from the Hereford Map.

According to Saint Anthony's biographer, the saint was tormented by the satyr and other beasts, which were demons in disguise. He emerged victorious. In fact, Saint Anthony helped convert the satyr and all of his kind to the Christian faith!

Closer to the era of the map itself, the traveler known as Sir John Mandeville also claimed to have penetrated the distant lands of Asia. We do not know who "Sir John" really was, only that the fourteenth-century travel guide he wrote provided a valuable source of information about the world. It exists in nearly three hundred manuscript copies and found its way into the libraries of nobles and princes. Unlike Anthony, Sir John was no saint—he was a traveler (perhaps an armchair traveler) whose insatiable curiosity about the world took him to the Holy Land and beyond, deep into the recesses of Asia. His guide describes a host of monstrous creatures he claimed to have encountered, including the Astomi, Pygmies, and Sciopods we see on the Hereford Map.

Sir John's text might disappoint readers looking for juicy tidbits about the monstrous races. He is dry and anthropologic, contenting himself with terse descriptions. Of the Sciopods, for example, Sir John says, "In that country be folk that have but one foot, and they go so blyve [quickly] that it is marvel. And the foot is so large, that it shadoweth all the body against the sun, when they will lie and rest them."[1] His description corresponds well enough to the Hereford Map's picture of the Sciopod shading himself with his giant foot. We are left to wonder, however, what it was like to come face to face (or foot to foot?) with such an unusual creature. Given the popularity of Sir John's travel guide, even his brief observations must have given medieval readers a vicarious thrill, as when we hear about distant sightings of Bigfoot today. He claimed to go where so many people in the medieval world could not.

But there is one place on the edge to which even Sir John did not go. As he traveled deeper into India, he came closer and closer to the most desired yet elusive site on earth. He approached Earthly Paradise. Today, we call this site the garden of Eden—the very place in which human life began. As we saw in chapter 3, in the Middle Ages, Eden was thought to have a physical location on earth. On maps, it appears at the top of the world, on the easternmost rim of Asia.

---

1. Mandeville, *Travels*, 105. While Mandeville places the Sciopods in Ethiopia, the Hereford Map shows them in Asia as well as Africa.

Although greatly revered, Earthly Paradise was also forbidden. We read in Genesis that, after expelling Adam and Eve, God "placed on the east side of the Garden of Eden cherubim and a flaming sword flashing back and forth to guard the way to the tree of life" (Gen 3:24). On the Hereford Map, Earthly Paradise is a walled garden with its gate resolutely shut. Adam and Eve, we recall, are driven from the garden, with no hope of reentry. Eden is off limits.

Eden's enclosure did not prevent medieval travelers from trying to reach it. Many accounts of their efforts have come down to us. Some travelers searched for but could not find the garden—according to some reports, it was hidden from human view. Yet Ranulf Higden, an English monk, wrote that witnesses had seen the garden of Eden. One of these was Johannes de Hese, a Dutch cleric, who claimed that he glimpsed Paradise from a distance as he traveled through the Far East in the late fourteenth century. Hese wrote, "And around the hour of vespers, when the sun goes down . . . the wall of Paradise can be seen in great clarity and beauty, like a star."[2]

A few intrepid travelers came as close as the four mighty rivers that flowed from Earthly Paradise into Asia. Here, their luck ran out. Of these travelers, Sir John Mandeville writes,

> Many great lords have assayed with great will, many times, for to pass by those rivers towards Paradise, with full great companies. But they might not speed in their voyage. And many died for weariness of rowing against those strong waves. And many of them became blind, and many deaf, for the noise of the water. And some were perished and lost within the waves. So that no mortal man may approach to that place, without special grace of God, so that of that place I can say you no more; and therefore, I shall hold me still, and return to that, that I have seen.[3]

Sir John's account makes clear the dangers of traveling to the edge. Even sacred sites, should they be located on the rim of the world, were full of risk. Take another look at Earthly Paradise in figure 11 of the previous chapter. As Adam and Eve are expelled from the garden, they begin heading south. They do not get far before they run into two monstrous creatures. The monsters have human bodies and canine heads, in the manner of the

---

2. Quoted in Westrem, *Broader Horizons*, 223.

3. Mandeville, *Travels*, 201–2.

creatures known as Cynocephali, or Dog-Heads. They raise their heads and howl, as if signaling the perils that await travelers to this forbidden zone.

The Hereford Map thus gives us a picture of a world encircled by taboo, by danger, by the unknown, by sin. The outer zone is summed up by four gold letters placed around the circumference of the map: MORS. These letters spell, in Latin, the word *death*. The rim of the earth reminds us that death is waiting, although hopefully in a distant place and time.

The Human Condition

I sympathize with the way that medieval Christians saw their world. On their maps, they pushed the monsters to the edges of existence, as if somehow the bad things of life could be kept away. Please don't misunderstand me. I do not sympathize with the prejudice and fear that led mapmakers to relegate "exotic" people to the edges of the earth. In fact, I struggle with this aspect of medieval geography. My study of medieval maps, however, has led me to believe that the monstrous races can also be interpreted symbolically. The monsters that lurk at the gate of Paradise, along with the word MORS that encircles the Hereford Map, tell us that these creatures have a cosmic meaning. They stand for the sin and evil that entered the world so soon after its creation. They indicate that the world is not an entirely safe place.

The fear of sin I understand. And I sympathize with the mapmakers' desire to distance sin and other dangers in our midst. This is a very human tendency. We don't want to think about our troubles. We *can't* think about them all the time. So we push them away. In the edge, we find an ingenious device for picturing and policing the danger zone of our world.

Yet the Hereford Map contains a reminder that we cannot escape this danger. When medieval Europeans looked at the edge of the map, they saw not only monsters. They also saw themselves. The map was displayed in Hereford Cathedral, and the city of Hereford is pictured in England, in the far northwest corner of the world (see fig. 10 in chapter 2). England was itself on the edge of the earth—in the danger zone, the same zone that housed the monstrous creatures and the forbidden garden of Eden.

In their texts, medieval British historians speak with anxiety about the geographical location of their homeland. They describe being cut off from the rest of civilization, referring to the British Isles as "pimples on the sphere of the earth" and "the boundaries of the world."[4] It surely was not

---

4. Mittman, *Maps and Monsters*, 20, 23.

only historians who felt this way. When ordinary pilgrims journeyed to Hereford Cathedral and found themselves face to face with the Hereford Map, they also came face to face with their existence on the edge. The city of Jerusalem, the center of the world and the heart of their faith, must have seemed a long way off.

The map thus makes a profound statement about the human condition. Life takes us to the edge; no one escapes the danger zone. "There is no safety in this world, no easy path to take, no convenient and comfortable way to live," notes Gerald Sittser, who has written about the journey of struggle in the Christian life. He goes on: "Though Christ has redeemed us from sin, defeated Satan and conquered death, he has not taken us out of this world."[5] Consequently, as we journey through the world, we know trouble. We know sickness, loneliness, and sorrow. We may feel, at times, that we are traveling in a dangerous and unknown land and that we will never find our way back to a safer place.

Our journey to the edge can be particularly painful when we go there of our own volition, as I do when I let my impatience with my daughter get the better of me. I become a monster in a monstrous land. At the edge, we taste the futility of our existence. We reap the consequences of sin. We have gone as far as we can go.

Grace at the Edge

Yet there is also a dose of grace at the world's end. We find it on the Ebstorf Map, a giant of a map—some twelve feet in diameter—made for a Benedictine convent in Germany around 1300.[6] We met this map briefly in chapter 2, where we examined its portrayal of Jerusalem. Like the Hereford Map, the Ebstorf Map pictures the forbidden garden at the top of the world and features monsters at the edges of the earth. In fact, its southern tip has twenty-four monstrous creatures, more than any surviving map from the Middle Ages. But take a closer look at the circumference of this map. The head, hands, and feet of Jesus peep out from behind the round image of the world. It is as though Jesus stands behind the earth, grasping it firmly in his hands (see fig. 2). He even holds the monstrous creatures; his left hand

5. Sittser, *Water from a Deep Well*, 74.

6. The Ebstorf Map was destroyed in 1943 and is known today through a full-size, hand-colored reproduction and other facsimiles. The illustrations in this book are taken from a facsimile of the map made by the German scholar Konrad Miller in 1896.

appears inside the boxed area that pictures a Troglodyte, a creature so fast that it could pounce atop its game (fig. 20).

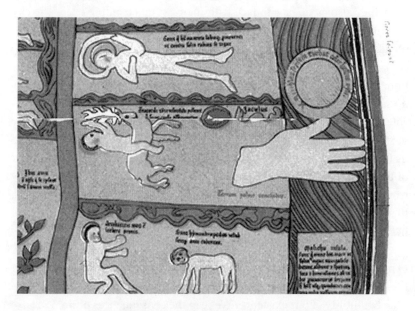

FIGURE 20. Jesus' hand holds a Troglodyte. The wound on his hand is not visible in this facsimile of the map. Detail from the Ebstorf Map.

An adjacent inscription reads, "He holds the earth in his hands."

Jesus' hands are distinctive in that, along with his feet, they bear wounds from the cross. The map thus presents an image of the crucified Christ. Jesus' wounds invite us to turn our attention to the center of the map, where, in the city of Jerusalem, he died and was resurrected. As we saw in chapter 2, the Ebstorf Map's picture of Jerusalem shows Jesus rising from the grave. He holds a banner of victory and stands with one foot inside the tomb and one foot out—he is earthly and heavenly at the same time (see fig. 7). Most medieval maps show Jerusalem by way of a cross, the crucifixion, or a church. The Ebstorf Map displays the resurrection and thereby emphasizes Jesus' victory. He has defeated the monsters of sin and death.

The Ebstorf Map thus portrays Jesus twice—at the edge, he holds the world, and at the center, he saves the world. This double image of Jesus makes a remarkable statement about God's care for all of humanity. Jesus is everywhere! The world is secure in his grasp. Humans may fail, but Jesus will never drop the ball, so to speak.

The map's double image of Jesus also provides a visual counterpart to the medieval theology of monsters. For the most part, the monstrous races stood for sin and moral depravity. Yet according to Saint Augustine, they could also tell people about God. Augustine theorized about the monsters in his magisterial history, *The City of God*. The monsters presented a real problem for the church. How could they be part of God's created order of the world, as maps showed them to be? Augustine tackled the problem head-on. As we saw in chapter 3, he said that the monstrous races descended, through Noah's sons, from Adam himself. They must, therefore, be human. They have souls and will be redeemed at the end of time, just like the rest of us. According to Augustine, the monsters' humanity meant that they could be saved.

Augustine's argument appears in visual form on a twelfth-century tympanum above the central portal of the Basilica of Saint Mary Magdalene in Vézelay. The main scene of the tympanum depicts the Pentecost and Mission of the Apostles. The apostles receive the Holy Spirit and, holding books, prepare to spread God's word to the ends of the earth (fig. 21).

FIGURE 21. The Pentecost and Mission of the Apostles. Tympanum above the central portal of the Basilica of Saint Mary Magdalene in Vézelay, ca. 1132.

Above and below this scene appear a variety of monstrous creatures poised to receive the good news. These creatures include the Cynocephali, or Dog-Heads, the Panotii (with giant ears), the Pygmies, and the Sciritae (noseless men). On the tympanum, as on medieval maps, the monstrous creatures occupy the boundaries of the image space; they are segregated from the heart of civilization (fig. 22).

FIGURE 22. Pygmies (one climbing a ladder to mount his horse) and Panotii (with large, winglike ears). Detail from the Vézelay tympanum.

But, spreading out from the center, the word still comes to them. As human beings, albeit strangely shaped ones, they are included in God's plan of salvation.[7]

Augustine's argument can also be seen on the Ebstorf Map. This map does not show the conversion of the monstrous races, as does (by implication) the Vézelay tympanum, but it does show God's compassion for them. Jesus wraps his wounded hands around the monsters and thereby includes them in the redemption of the world.

The Latin word for monster, *monstrum*, derives from *monstrare*, which means to show or to demonstrate. In the *City of God*, Augustine plays on this etymology. The purpose of a *monstrum* is to *monstrare*, he says: "Yet,

---

7. There are many scholarly interpretations of the Vézelay tympanum. In my discussion, I am following the one advanced by Friedman, *Monstrous Races*, 77–79.

for our part, these things which happen contrary to nature . . . and are called monsters, phenomena, portents, prodigies, ought to demonstrate, portend, predict that God will bring to pass what He has foretold regarding the bodies of men, no difficulty preventing Him, no law of nature prescribing to Him His limit."[8] To Augustine, the monstrous creatures demonstrate the power of God to save humankind. No person lies beyond his reach. God redeems the edge, making it a place of miracles as well as monsters.

The Challenge for Our World

In the Ebstorf Map is a message of compassion for our world. When I look at this image of Jesus embracing the earth, I am always reminded of the song my children love to sing: "He's Got the Whole World in His Hands." In fact, the map makes me feel like a kid again. I see Jesus with his arms spread wide, and I want to run to him! In his spiritual autobiography, *The Confessions*, Augustine said that God cares for each one of us as though we were the only one in his care.[9] Some people paraphrase this idea by saying that God loves each of us like an only child. He is a parent waiting for his one and only to run into his arms and feel safe again. He waits to gather us up and take us home.

In the charm of this map's image of a savior embracing the edge, there is also a challenge. Can we see the edge of our world—our wilderness—as a place to run to Jesus? Can we see it as an opportunity rather than a loss? I have always tended to see the edge in terms of the Hereford Map—as a place of danger and death, a wilderness to be avoided at all costs (if such a thing were possible). I don't want to paint a bad picture of the Hereford Map. It contains much valuable information for us, not least the metaphor it provides for our struggles in the world. But we need the vision of the Ebstorf Map, too. This map shows that the edge is part of our journey with Jesus. It is where we come face to face with our need for him.

It is not always comfortable to admit our need. It makes us feel weak and vulnerable. We are exposed, with nowhere to hide, and most of us don't like that. Yet our need can bring us closer to Jesus. The Bible affirms that we will find Jesus in our time of trouble. He came to give us life, helping us live abundantly in the midst of our hardships (John 10:10). And he died to save us from sin and death (John 3:16). If we seek Jesus in our struggles, we will

8. Augustine, *City of God*, 21.8 (Dods, 778).

9. Augustine, *Confessions*, 3.11.19 (Outler, 74).

surely find him there. We may, in fact, discover that we turn to him more when we are struggling. When we can do little for ourselves, we are forced to rely on Jesus. On the edge, we meet the savior who suffered and died for us, and we let him wrap his arms around us.

Some Christians have courted the edge specifically to meet Jesus. I think, for example, of the Hereford Map's reference to Saint Anthony. In the early Christian period, Saint Anthony and other desert fathers retreated to the Egyptian wilderness to come closer to Christ. Their deliberate isolation from more civilized areas is often pinpointed as the beginning of monasticism. For the desert fathers, the edge was not just a symbol. They entered a real wilderness in which physical hardship became a way of life.

In reading the stories and sayings of the desert fathers, it becomes clear that these spiritual fathers and mothers did not just endure the edge. They sought Jesus there. Sometimes they "asked for trouble," treating physical and spiritual struggle as a refining fire for the soul. According to one story, a sickly old man was "grievously troubled" when one year he did not fall ill as usual; he saw this as a kind of abondonment, saying, "the Lord has left me, and has not visited me."[10] In most of the Bible studies I've attended, our prayer time is filled with requests for healing. Yet this man felt the presence of Jesus in his sickness. Another desert father, the abbot Abraham, summed up his way of life by saying, "we have joy in this desolation."[11]

These kinds of affirmations may be beyond most of us today. I certainly am not to the point of taking joy in my struggles and infirmities. I don't seek trouble, even for the sake of spiritual growth. But I see value in the stories of the desert fathers: through their experiences, we learn that the edge is a place where we can meet Jesus. We can know his joy in the midst of hardship.

From our own era comes another story that seems closer to home. This story concerns Father Thomas Keating, a monk and spiritual leader at the forefront of the discipline of centering prayer. We might not think of prayer as a place where we would run into trouble. But really, trouble can come to us anywhere. When a nun who took Father Keating's workshop worried that she had had ten thousand distracting thoughts during her prayer, Father Keating replied, "How lovely! Ten thousand opportunities to return to God!"[12]

10. Chadwick, *Western Asceticism*, 94.
11. Quoted in Waddell, *Desert Fathers*, 160.
12. Quoted in Bourgeault, *Centering Prayer*, 24.

As in prayer, so in life. We can always return to God—even ten thousand times. Life gives us many moments that threaten to do us in. We fall ill. We become overwhelmed. We lose patience. We sin—and sin again. Each of our difficult moments can be an opportunity to let Jesus gather us into his arms. How do we seize this opportunity? The Ebstorf Map shows that Jesus has positioned himself on the edge, in the very darkness of our lives—he is there for us to find. So we begin by opening our eyes and seeing Jesus in our world. We realize that he is present in the troubling times as well as the good. We remember that he died to save the world from death, both physical and spiritual. Perhaps, following Father Keating's example, we say a prayer to redirect our thoughts to Jesus. It might be a prayer for help. We might need to ask forgiveness. Or it might be nothing more than breathing Jesus' name—a simple form of acknowledgment of our desperate need for him. Then we rest in his embrace.

The Ebstorf Map can be a companion in our need. Like a good pastor, it instructs us with tenderness and compassion. It invites us to be enfolded in the arms of Jesus, and it challenges us to reorder our world. When we contemplate the map's picture of Jesus on the edge, we realize that there are places we cannot and perhaps should not avoid in our journey of faith. We have to give our world—all of it—to Jesus. No part of the world is beyond his power to tame. Just think: if Jesus can save the monstrous creatures that roam the edge, surely he can save the likes of you and me!

Reflections and Practices

- Recall a situation that has taken you to the edge recently, perhaps even today. Can you see Jesus there with you?

- Read Psalm 139:7–10. Meditate on the fact that no matter what scary places we visit in our lives, God's hand will always lead us and hold us.

- Turn to the illustration of the Ebstorf Map in figure 2. Look at the edge of the map and see Jesus' arms encircling the world. See how he holds you, even when you are on the edge. Take a few minutes to rest in Jesus' embrace.

- Pray that Jesus will meet you on the edge as you go forward on your journey of faith.

5

Journeying to Jerusalem

Have you ever noticed how often the Christian faith is described in terms of movement? In his letters to the early church, the Apostle Paul peppers his remarks with metaphors of motion. The most unusual, to my eyes, is his description of self-discipline as a boxing match (1 Cor 9:26–27). More frequently, Paul speaks of running a race (Gal 2:2; 5:7; 1 Cor 9:24) or straining forward, of pressing on toward the goal to win the prize (Phil 3:14).

Over the years, Christians have invented new metaphors for the life of faith. We talk about our spiritual journey. Our walk with God. Our earthly pilgrimage. Even our leaps of faith. As Christians, we are going somewhere!

At least, we're supposed to be. If we are honest, most of us admit to stumbling in our walk of faith. We encounter setbacks, take lengthy detours, and meet roadblocks. We go the wrong way down one-way streets. Sometimes it feels as though we're crawling instead of running a glorious race—let alone winning any sort of prize.

Perhaps we can turn to medieval Christians for help. The great image of medieval spirituality, as we have been exploring in this book, was nothing other than a map. Maps of the Middle Ages spurred their users onward. Full of sacred sites, they invited people to dream, plan, and imagine their journey with God. Some journeys were real, such as the pilgrimages that medieval Christians took to shrines the world over. Others might have been journeys of the heart. With their network of paths leading all over the Christian world, such maps are ideal vehicles for exploring the imagery of movement we find in the Bible and other descriptions of spiritual life.

For this reason, the next three chapters will explore our spiritual journey as figured on medieval world maps—primarily the Hereford Map, but also, in chapter 7, a much smaller map known as the Psalter Map. Through the maps' imagery of movement, we find encouragement to press on in our journey. This is essential; we have to keep moving forward. "To stand still in the spiritual life is to be in imminent danger of regressing," write John P. H. Clark and Rosemary Dorward.[1] Medieval maps can help us in our effort to keep going—despite setbacks, despite hardships. Through these maps, we learn to persevere in our goal.

Are you ready to travel? You'll need your cloak, staff, and scrip, because as we move forward, we'll be doing so in the guise of medieval pilgrims. We're going to hit the road to find God in the holiest place on earth. You'll also need a willingness to brave danger and hardship; our pilgrimage path leads through difficult territory. With the Hereford Map as a guide, however, we can say with certainty that we will reach our goal. We'll arrive, spent but victorious, at the center of our world and our faith. We'll meet Jesus in the place where he awaits each one of us.

The Quest of a Lifetime

My introduction to medieval pilgrimage came by way of the *Canterbury Tales*, assigned by my ninth-grade English teacher. I don't recall much from this early reading of Chaucer's poem. Certain details, however, and especially certain characters, have stayed with me throughout my engagement with the Middle Ages. One of these is the Wife of Bath, she of the weighty wimples and even weightier past. The Wife of Bath had a mixed history, to say the least. She had had five husbands and, just as surprising, had been on seven sacred journeys (not counting her present journey to Canterbury, the subject of Chaucer's poem). The woman was addicted to pilgrimage. It strikes me that if Chaucer had sent the Wife of Bath to Hereford Cathedral, she would have had a good deal to say about its map: she had traveled much of its world in pursuit of her devotion.

On the Hereford Map, the Wife of Bath could have pointed out the three greatest shrines of the Middle Ages, all of which she had visited. Let's take a brief look at the first two. On the Mediterranean Sea lies the city of Rome, home to the sanctuaries of Saints Peter and Paul, as well as numerous early Christian martyrs. On the map, Rome is the second largest city on the continent of Europe (fig. 23).

1. Clark and Dorward, "Introduction," in Hilton, *Scale of Perfection*, 44.

FIGURE 23. City of Rome (in the center of the image). Detail from the Hereford Map.

In the Jubilee year of 1300, about when the Hereford Map was made, hundreds of thousands of pilgrims traveled there to receive absolution and indulgences.

Farther west, at the bottom of the map, we see the church of Saint James in Compostela, Spain (fig. 24). It was said to house the remains of Saint James the Greater and was the most popular pilgrimage destination in Europe outside of Rome. The Hereford Map privileges this shrine by showing several towns along the Somport pass, a well-traveled pilgrimage route that wound across the Pyrenees from southern France to Compostela. The Wife of Bath, or perhaps another pilgrim standing before the map, could have relived or planned her journey to Saint James, which was located, like Hereford itself, on the edge of the world.

The premier pilgrimage destination of the Middle Ages lay not at the world's edge but at its center—Jerusalem, the site of Jesus' last days and of his crucifixion and resurrection. The Wife of Bath had journeyed there three times—a lot for a medieval traveler, especially an English one. England, we recall, was located on the edge of the medieval world. Pilgrims from this remote land had a long way to go. But, the fictional Wife of Bath aside, we know of real pilgrims who went two and three times to Jerusalem. It was worth a repeat trip.

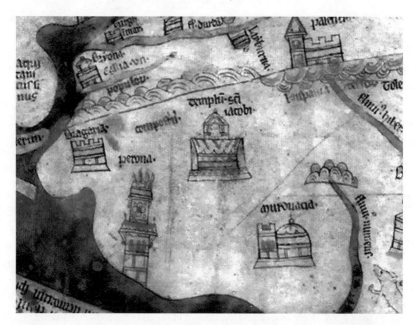

FIGURE 24. Church of Saint James in Compostela, Spain (in the center of the image). Detail from the Hereford Map.

It may not look like it from the Hereford Map. Jerusalem lies at the map's center, but the city is small and not very detailed. As we saw in chapter 2, Jerusalem appears as a circular, walled city with four towers and four gates (see fig. 5). These towers and gates point inward to two concentric circles surrounded by eight smaller circles. These circles don't look like much to us, but they would have made a pilgrim's heart beat a little faster. They are probably meant to represent a domed edifice with a circular colonnade, an arrangement that recalls the site of Jesus' tomb in Jerusalem's premier destination, the Church of the Holy Sepulcher.

This church was the ultimate goal of the Jerusalem pilgrimage, and it has an eventful history that itself began with a sacred journey. According to legend, the Emperor Constantine's mother, Helena, visited Jerusalem in the fourth century. After determining the location of Jesus' tomb, she demolished a pagan temple that had been built on the site and found the three crosses of Calvary buried deep beneath it. She was able to discern the cross of Christ, or the "true cross," when it healed a diseased woman. Helena had Constantine build a basilica on this site. The basilica, completed in 335, became known as the Church of the Holy Sepulcher. It enclosed the shrines of Jesus' crucifixion and burial, as well as other sites from Jesus' last days (fig. 25).

FIGURE 25. Main entrance to the Church of the Holy Sepulcher, Jerusalem.

The crucifixion itself, as we saw in chapter 2, rises from the city of Jerusalem on the Hereford Map. At its base is the label "Mount Calvary." Together, image and label recall the site that Helena discovered and that Constantine made into a shrine. On the map, Jesus' cross not only centers the world. It also beckons pilgrims to come and worship at the very place that it does so.

With its domed church and vision of the cross, the Hereford Map allows us to see Jerusalem with a pilgrim's mindset. In previous chapters, we explored Jerusalem as the center of a worldview and the center of history. But Jerusalem was more than a symbol or a concept. It was also an earthly destination. A real city, one with centuries of history, it represented the pinnacle of the medieval pilgrimage experience. Not as many pilgrims went to Jerusalem as to Rome and Compostela. Staying in Europe was, obviously, easier than traveling to the Holy Land. Yet of all shrines, Jerusalem brought Christians closest to Jesus, the center of their faith. In this city, their physical journey met their heart's yearning for Christ.

Jerusalem allowed Western Christians to experience the humanity of Jesus in ways they could not do at home. Late medieval spirituality placed a strong emphasis on Christ's body and on his suffering, more so than many of our spiritual traditions do today. At my church, for example, we talk a good deal about the cross, and we acknowledge Jesus' suffering. We don't usually go into the physical details, however. Medieval Christians did. They contemplated and prayed to Jesus' wounds. They painted the wounds life-size, indicating the measurements of each one. They also visualized and meditated upon each step of Jesus' journey to the cross.

In Jerusalem, Christians could suffer and journey with Jesus. Pilgrims visited many sites associated with Jesus' final days, but their walk of sorrow culminated in the Church of the Holy Sepulcher. It is difficult to imagine the respectable but pragmatic Wife of Bath in this church. For flesh-and-blood pilgrims, its shrines prompted tearful and heartfelt devotion. In its candlelit interior, pilgrims went from shrine to shrine, sometimes barefoot. They visited the place where Jesus was stripped of his clothing, the pillar where he was scourged, the rock of Calvary, the slab where his body was anointed, and his tomb—the sepulcher itself.

As they took this holy tour, pilgrims not only contemplated Jesus' suffering. They also tried to participate in it. They shed tears. They begged for visions. They touched the rock of Jesus' tomb and thrust their head inside a fissure beside the socket hole of the cross. In their desire to imitate Jesus, some pilgrims even washed the feet of the poor or flagellated themselves. Their journey to Jerusalem was more than well-intentioned tourism. It was a quest to Jesus and an effort to be more like him.

A Sack of Patience

Pilgrimage also describes our daily quest as Christians. Each of us has, in the words of Saint Bonaventure, an "interior Jerusalem" to which we travel.[2] Like medieval pilgrims, we're trying to close the distance between Jesus and us. We want to be closer to him and to become more Christlike each day. So we make the journey to Jesus, the center of our world, the very center of our heart. We make it as many times as our savior beckons us.

What can we learn from medieval pilgrims who walked and rode and sailed the long way to the center of the world? We learn that it costs everything—sometimes literally. More than one pilgrim arrived in Jerusalem completely broke, unable to pay the tax required for entering the city. So it is with the voyage to our interior Jerusalem. It requires all of us—our minds, our souls, our hearts. As we explore the historical details

2. Bonaventure, *Soul's Journey into God*, 7.1 (Cousins, 110).

of medieval pilgrimage below, think about your journey to Jesus. The accounts are sobering, but as pilgrims on our own road of faith, we need to hear them.[3]

Sometimes, our age romanticizes pilgrimage. In glossy photos and travel guides, it symbolizes the call of the open road (fig. 26).

FIGURE 26. A pilgrim on the road in Spain.

We think of a journey, even a sacred one, and we think new scenery, new discoveries, and a welcome change of pace. Medieval pilgrimage, however, went beyond wanderlust or the desire for a good adventure. Adventure waited, certainly. As they traveled, pilgrims encountered new sights. If they went to Jerusalem by boat, they usually passed through the city of Venice, bustling with ships and commerce. There, many pilgrims caught their first glimpse of the Mediterranean Sea. In the Holy Land, they admired the bazaars, puzzled at the foreign customs, and marveled at a land steeped in history.

But these distractions do not mask the difficulty of the journey. A pilgrim traveling from England to Jerusalem made a voyage from the edge of the world to its very center. It may have been an adventure, but not one to embark upon lightly. Pilgrims left behind everything familiar—family,

---

3. Reading about medieval pilgrimage is entertaining and enlightening. The literature is vast. Sources that informed my discussion of pilgrimage in this chapter include Chareyron, *Pilgrims to Jerusalem*; Sumption, *Pilgrimage*; Webb, *Pilgrims and Pilgrimage*; and Prescott, *Friar Felix at Large*.

livelihood, language, and culture. They took with them a big purse and a lot of hope. The fourteenth-century Irish pilgrim Symon Semeonis said, "Every man who undertakes the journey to Our Lord's Sepulcher needs three sacks: a sack of patience, a sack of silver, and a sack of faith."[4]

From France, the first leg of the Jerusalem pilgrimage progressed by foot, perhaps by horse for wealthier travelers. If going by way of Venice, the most popular route, pilgrims first crossed the Alps. They had to rely upon local guides since the mountain paths were often buried by snow. Sometimes the snow covered a layer of mud and deep holes, causing horses to sink up to their bellies.

Pilgrims could rest their weary feet when they finally got on a boat for the last leg of the journey to the Holy Land. Yet sea voyages, too, were uncertain, dependent upon good winds, a strong stomach, and the absence of pirates. Pilgrims slept with rats, ate spoiled food, and witnessed burials at sea.

We must not forget the human element. At any point during the various legs of their trip, pilgrims could be swindled, robbed, or attacked. They might lose money exchanging their currency for Venetian ducats (the Venetians held a monopoly on sea travel to the Holy land and could dictate their terms). They could be cheated by the captain of their ship or made to bunk with unsympathetic roommates who were sick all night, or who snored, or who stepped on them in an effort to get fresh air. Sometimes they were obliged to engage in hand-to-hand fighting with pirates. In the eleventh century, several thousand German pilgrims were attacked by Arabs as they journeyed overland to Jerusalem. One gets the sense that anything could happen at any time. The lack of control over many parts of the voyage must have been unsettling.

What would you do if your spouse or child declared the intent to set out on a journey like this? Would you yourself take the risk? In the Middle Ages, family members sometimes begged a departing pilgrim not to go. Before setting out, especially to the Holy Land, many pilgrims drew up their wills or stipulated the length of time after which their spouse could remarry should they fail to return.

Even upon arrival in the long-awaited land, pilgrims' troubles did not cease. In fact, they multiplied, especially for those traveling in the later Middle Ages. In the mid-thirteenth century, the political situation changed in Jerusalem. When, after about six weeks of sea travel, pilgrims finally set

---

4. Quoted in Chareyron, *Pilgrims to Jerusalem*, 16.

foot in the Holy Land, they found themselves in occupied territory. From 1291, when the city of Acre fell to the Mamluk army, the Christian West no longer controlled the Holy Land. Jerusalem itself had fallen in 1244, about half a century before the Hereford Map was made.

Egyptian and Mamluk sultans now ruled over Jerusalem. They tolerated pilgrims from Europe, but their forbearance did not always extend to good treatment. Upon arriving in the port city of Jaffa, pilgrims were kept on board their ship or in holding cells until their "visas" and letters of permission were sorted out. Afterwards, a difficult journey inland ensued. One English pilgrim wrote that, along the road from Jaffa to Jerusalem, Arabs "lay hidden in caves and crevices, waiting day and night for people travelling in small parties or straggling behind their groups. At one moment they are everywhere, the next they are gone. Their presence is felt by every one who passes on that fatal road."[5]

Once they reached Jerusalem, pilgrims could not visit all the sacred sites they had journeyed such a great distance to see. They saw the Church of the Holy Sepulcher, of course. Yet other sites, like the chapel where the Pentecost occurred, had been destroyed, or, as in the case of Saint Anne's house, turned into mosques. Friar Felix Fabri, a fifteenth-century pilgrim, writes that a Muslim official chased him out of the Fountain of the Virgin, located in a cave at the foot of Mt. Sion, and then fought with another member of his traveling party.

Fortunately, pilgrims did have advocates. In the fourteenth century, Franciscan friars organized the Jerusalem pilgrimage experience. These friars, the only Western Christians allowed to reside in the Holy Land, acted as tour guides, taking the pilgrims to all the sacred sites. The friars also provided meals and took care of any pilgrims who fell ill. There was just one catch. Pilgrims were more or less tied to their Franciscan guides. They did not have the freedom to move about on their own, and this in itself must have been a constant reminder that enemies now held the most sacred sites in Christendom.

Can you imagine the frustration for travel-worn pilgrims? A grueling voyage is endured, and hope with difficulty sustained, all for the privilege of worshipping on enemy ground. Attaining the promised land did not guarantee safety for medieval pilgrims. It did not guarantee ease. At the very heart of the Christian faith, trouble had to be dodged at every turn.

---

5. Quoted in Sumption, *Pilgrimage*, 184. This pilgrim wrote in 1102, a century and a half before Jerusalem was taken. Evidently, dangers existed even then.

Is It Worth It?

Pilgrims had to really want this "holy journey," as they called the voyage to Jerusalem. Their destination had to be worth risking everything, life and limb included. Was it worth it to sleep with rats and eat spoiled food? Was it worth it to be harassed by the locals, or to be locked in a holding cell, or to do battle within the sacred city itself?

Let's allow a pilgrim to answer this question. In 1026, the Abbot Richard of St. Vannes journeyed to Jerusalem. Richard's biographer describes his reaction when, "after many sorts of peril," he finally set foot in the Holy Land:

> Oh, what was his love towards God! What the exultation of his contrite and humbled spirit! What the jubilation of his heart, when he saw himself present where Christ was born, where he suffered, where he was buried, where his feet last stood when he ascended into heaven. Everywhere that he prayed, he soaked the ground with tears, the cry of his heart rose up to the Lord, his body sank down, his spirit rose aloft. He spent the night continually in vigils, he wore down his body with fasts, never without tears, never without prayers; his whole being exulted in the Lord, but he cloaked the gladness of his mind with serenity of countenance . . . [6]

Was the journey worth it? Abbot Richard seems to have thought so.

Four centuries later, pilgrims' responses had not changed much. In 1480, Friar Felix Fabri reported that, before being shown to their lodgings, pilgrims were led to the door of the Church of the Holy Sepulcher. When told what the building was, men sobbed and women shrieked as if in labor.

The highlight of the late medieval pilgrimage was an overnight vigil inside the church, which took place on three separate nights. Pilgrims were locked (voluntarily) in the church by their Muslim hosts. Inside, the Franciscans led them from shrine to shrine, saying prayers and singing; the pilgrims went barefoot and carried candles. High Mass was said at daybreak, after which the Muslims unceremoniously kicked the pilgrims out of the church. This vigil, including the occasionally rough treatment by the Muslims in charge, was undertaken in imitation of the crucifixion. Margery Kempe, an early fifteenth-century pilgrim, even claimed to have been granted a vision of the crucified Christ during her vigil. Speaking of herself in the third person, she describes her reaction to this vision:

6. Quoted in Webb, *Pilgrims and Pilgrimage*, 40.

> And when, through dispensation of the high mercy of our Sovereign Saviour Jesus Christ, it was granted this creature to see so vividly his precious tender body hanging upon the cross . . . then she fell down and cried out with a loud voice, writhing and twisting her body amazingly from side to side, spreading her arms asunder as if she would have died. Nor could she prevent herself from crying, nor control these bodily contortions, because of the fire of love that burnt so fervently in her soul with pure pity and compassion.[7]

All these tears and contortions may not be to modern taste, but they describe medieval faith perfectly. Medieval spirituality was sometimes noisy; it could be emotional; it did not particularly care that others might be watching. In fact, one gets the sense that pilgrims wanted others to see their shrieks and groans. They recorded their emotional responses to Jerusalem because readers of their travel narratives expected to hear about them.

I want to hear about them, too, mostly to be reminded of an important part of the Jerusalem pilgrimage—its climax. When the journey to Jerusalem comes to a close, it closes in on Jesus. Pilgrims' cries and shrieks represent the sought-after culmination of an arduous voyage. Decorum didn't matter. Experiencing Jesus did. In pilgrims' emotional displays, we see the heart bursting open because it has finally reached its goal.

Is this true of our own hearts? Does our whole being exult, as did Abbot Richard's, when we make the journey to Jesus? Does our soul burn, like Margery Kempe's, with a "fire of love" for the Lord? Is the pilgrimage worth it?

The Challenge for Our World

Every day, I ask myself if it's worth it. Because every day, Jesus beckons me. He calls me to make my pilgrimage to the cross. Am I up to this journey? Unlike a medieval pilgrimage, it is not physically arduous. I go to Jesus in my heart, not in the saddle or a sailing vessel. I follow him while sitting at my computer, taking care of my children, going to church, driving my car (no horses sinking up to their bellies in mud for me!). Despite my ease of bodily movement, the heart's journey to Jesus is by far the most difficult trip I have ever taken.

---

7. Kempe, *Book of Margery Kempe*, 38.

As I journey, I use a map—the Hereford Map, of course. Looking at the map, I imagine myself as an English pilgrim on the edge of the world. I see Jerusalem gleaming in the distance. The map shows me that I have a long way to travel. But because I want to be where Jesus is, I go. I say farewell to my habits and inclinations, and hopefully to my sin, which is sorry to see me leave. I die a little.

Then I set out. The way is difficult, and it is long. I miss those habits and sins I left behind. Many times, I am tempted to turn back. Sometimes, in fact, I do, and I have to begin my voyage all over again. When I am finally on the road, a thousand sights distract me. Friar Felix said that the pilgrims with whom he traveled were especially drawn to the Dome of the Rock, a mosque that had nothing to do with the sacred sites of Christianity. Glittering temples attract me, too. Pride. Vanity. Wealth. I'll go after them all.

As I get closer to Jerusalem, I enter enemy territory. Here, the real battle begins. I am accosted by the infidels of my heart, who would do anything to keep me from my goal. They don't want me to pray. They don't want me to pick up my Bible. They don't want me to confess my sins or sing songs of praise. So my enemies shout at me and tell me to turn back. They persuade me, almost, that I'll never be able to pay the price to enter the sacred city of Jerusalem. They are right about that. Someone else had to pay for me.

Finally, I enter the city, and I kneel—or rather, collapse—at the cross of Christ. My daily pilgrimage has taught me why Christians speak so frequently of kneeling at the foot of the cross. It's because, exhausted by the journey to Jerusalem, we can no longer stand. The worst of it is that I arrive with nothing. No money to pay the tax, no place to stay, no offering to leave. Walter Hilton, an Augustinian mystic of the fourteenth century, said, "Just as a true pilgrim going to Jerusalem leaves behind him house and land, wife and children, and makes himself poor and bare of all that he has in order to travel light and without hindrance, so if you want to be a spiritual pilgrim you are to make yourself naked of all that you have . . ."[8] To journey to Jerusalem is to arrive with nothing, so that Jesus can give us everything.

The cross at the center of the Hereford Map reminds me that Jesus really does give us everything. The pilgrimage to Jerusalem may be arduous, but our Lord has done the truly difficult work already. He does what we cannot do ourselves: he saves us. He restores us. He bestows upon us endless streams of grace and mercy. When he beckons, we cannot stay where

---

8. Hilton, *Scale of Perfection*, 229.

we are; we cannot linger on the edges of the earth. We must go to him, running or walking or crawling as best we can. Our faith is a continual journey to Jerusalem, to be filled by Jesus Christ.

I like to think of the Hereford Map as a guide for our journey. It provides not a roadmap—our heart already knows the way—but an exercise in focusing on our goal. If we spend some time with the map, letting our gaze be drawn again and again to the city at its center, we learn to keep our eyes on the prize. We cut out distractions, even supposedly worthy ones, such as our past sins and our ongoing need for confession. "Trust firmly that you are on the road," Walter Hilton advises, "and you need no more ransacking of your confession for what is past: keep on your way and think of Jerusalem."[9] If we are thinking more about Jesus and less about the many things that slow us down, our journey will be eased. We can collapse the distance between Jesus and us.

When we finally reach our destination, we may feel like those medieval pilgrims who erupted in noisy tears and shouts. We may be bowled over by the beauty of Jerusalem. The difficulties of our journey fall away, and our hearts swell with praise. When Augustine of Hippo addressed God in the *Confessions*, he wrote, "I shall go into my own little room [the heart] and sing love songs to Thee, groaning unutterable groanings during my pilgrimage, recalling in my heart the Jerusalem to which my heart has been uplifted, Jerusalem my homeland, Jerusalem my mother, and Thee ruling over it . . ."[10]

In Jerusalem, we go into the room of our heart, where Jesus is waiting. Jesus, who fills us up. Jesus, who uplifts us. Jesus, who gives us everything. Yes, the journey is worth it.

Reflections and Practices

- Consider some of the metaphors of movement commonly used to describe the Christian faith: a race, a journey, a walk, a straining forward, a leap of faith. Which metaphors speak to your faith experience the most?

- What are some of the roadblocks in your daily journey to Jerusalem—to Jesus Christ? How might imagining your journey as a pilgrimage help you meet and overcome these hurdles?

9. Ibid., 231.

10. Augustine, *Confessions*, 12.16.23 (Bourke, 385).

- The Hereford Map provides a good exercise in keeping our eyes on the prize (see Phil 3:14). On the image of the Hereford Map in figure 1, find Jerusalem, at the center of the world. Use the map to focus for a few minutes on Jerusalem and the cross of Christ. When your gaze wanders to other places on the map, bring it back to the center. Keep your eyes on the prize!

6

Journeying through Life

At the bottom of the Hereford Map, just below the round image of the world, a man on horseback rides a magnificent stallion (fig. 27). The man is unnamed and unidentified. Scholars have long debated the identity of this mysterious figure. Is he Bishop Thomas of Cantilupe, whose remains lay inside the same church that housed the map? Or Alexander the Great and his beloved steed Bucephalus? My favorite interpretation suggests that this figure is an Everyman who prepares to go forth on the journey of life. He looks up at the world and gestures to us, inviting us to take this journey ourselves.

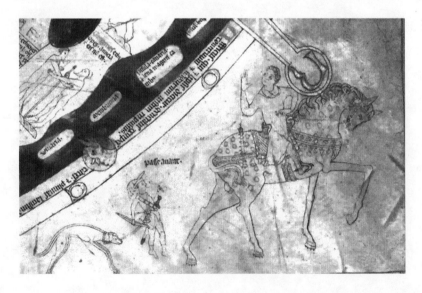

FIGURE 27. Everyman on horseback at the bottom of the Hereford Map.

What does the journey of life look like for you? Along what kind of path do you ride? Most of our travel narratives make life sound like a daunting trek indeed. We speak of struggling to keep up with the pace of life. Or of feeling stalled. We take a wrong turn here and hit a dead end there. Life has its ups and downs, we say, as if it were a mountainous path. These images are born of our anxiety about life and our fears for the future. They confirm, as if we didn't already know, just how rocky our road can be.

We need a road that offers a way through the rocks, a road that offers hope amidst the difficulties of life. The Hereford Map invites us to travel just such a road. We hear it described by the character of the Parson in Chaucer's *Canterbury Tales*:

> Now, at the end of our journey, I will bring matters to a conclusion.
> May the Saviour guide me and inspire me to lead you to Jerusalem.
> Our pilgrimage on earth is an image of the glorious pilgrimage to
> the celestial city.[1]

Our routes on earth, the Parson says, are but shadows of the larger path we take to our heavenly home. Life is itself a sacred journey—a pilgrimage. It encompasses our birth, our baptism and growth in Christ, and all the myriad experiences that fill up our days and years until we reach the end of the road. And what a glorious end it is!

In this chapter, we will explore the Hereford Map as a vast landscape through which we travel this road. We will be pilgrims once again, this time on the long and winding path of our life in Christ. As we go along, the map teaches us new metaphors that help define our journey as one of purpose and promise. Our path is by no means easy, but we can find flowers amidst the rocks.

Let us then follow Everyman into the landscape of the map. "Travel through the world!" this figure seems to say. He knows that if we follow the pilgrimage of life, it will take us where we want to go. It will lead us all the way home.

Peregrini on the Path

Everyman takes his journey by horseback at the foot of the Hereford Map. He must have been wealthy. Most pilgrims, as we saw in chapter 5, traveled by foot and by sea. Perhaps for this reason, walking and sailing shaped

---

1. Chaucer, *Canterbury Tales*, 434.

the way that medieval Christians saw the journey of life. We are invited to travel by both means on the Hereford Map.

We take the first part of our pilgrimage on foot. Our path leads through a rather harsh landscape—the wilderness. We will be journeying with the Israelites, the children of God who walked from Egypt to the promised land. The Israelites' journey—the exodus—takes place in the upper part of the Hereford Map, in the area surrounding the Red Sea. If you were standing in front of the map, you would find this one of the easiest places to spot. The Red Sea lives up to its name: it is colored red, a bright gash that digs into the earth.

The exodus grabs our attention in another way. Of all journeys on the map, it is the only one marked in ink (fig. 28).

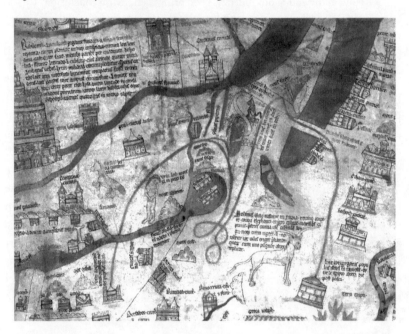

FIGURE 28. Exodus route. The route begins in the lower right, at the "granaries of Joseph." Note the phoenix perched below the parted Red Sea and, below the phoenix, the eale. Detail from the Hereford Map.

You can see, in figure 28, that the mapmaker(s) drew a line connecting the relevant sites in this journey, similar to the highlighted line that marks a route on a GPS today. This line invites us to follow the Israelites' path from beginning to end—perhaps even to walk it with our finger. It provides our first clue that the exodus is meant to guide us on our own journey through the world.

The Israelites' route begins in Ramses, close to the pyramids or, as the map calls them, the "granaries of Joseph." It then crosses the Red Sea, which has been miraculously parted. Following along, we see Moses receiving the tablets of the law atop Mt. Sinai and the Israelites worshiping the golden calf below. The path then takes several loops and turns before passing the Dead Sea, in which are visible the ruins of Sodom and Gomorrah. Lot's wife stands nearby, turned to a pillar of salt as she glances back at the destroyed cities. Finally, the Israelites cross the Jordan River and arrive in Jericho.

As we follow this extraordinary route, we get more than a lesson in Old Testament geography. We meet a surprising sight and receive a gift of grace. The clue to this surprise is found in the giant bird perched alongside the Exodus route—a bird as large as Mt. Sinai itself. This bird is the phoenix. According to medieval lore, only one phoenix existed at a time. Every five hundred years, it built a nest of spices and flapped its wings until it burst into flames. Another phoenix rose from the ashes to repeat the cycle.

The phoenix introduces us to the wonders of medieval Asia. Like Africa, the continent of Asia boasted amazing sights. Near Ramses, for example, we see another marvel of Asia, the eale. This animal, the map's legend tells us, had a horse's body, an elephant's tail, and marvelous horns that could rotate in different directions.

The phoenix can be called marvelous in another sense. Because of its powers of regeneration, medieval writers viewed it as a symbol of the resurrection. Its presence along the exodus route deepens the meaning of this Old Testament event. The phoenix becomes an ingenious way to show, in pictorial form, the foreshadowing of which Paul speaks in his first letter to the Corinthians:

> For I do not want you to be ignorant of the fact, brothers and sisters, that our ancestors were all under the cloud and that they all passed through the sea. They were all baptized into Moses in the cloud and in the sea. They all ate the same spiritual food and drank the same spiritual drink; for they drank from the spiritual rock that accompanied them, and that rock was Christ. (1 Cor 10:1–4)

Paul describes the Israelites' journey as a baptism into Jesus Christ. It is one of the many instances in which Old Testament events prefigure the coming of the savior. The phoenix, which looks innocuous yet resonates with resurrection, recalls Paul's interpretation of the exodus. It turns the

Israelites' trek into a journey that every Christian takes—our walk to salvation in Christ.

Each of us walks this walk. From the moment God calls us out of captivity to the day we stand before his throne, we journey through the wilderness of this world. The Israelites walked to Jericho, but we are on our way to Jerusalem, at the center of the map. With every step we take, we get closer and closer to the home God has prepared for us.

As travelers headed to Jerusalem, we are, of course, pilgrims. In chapter 5, we examined the Jerusalem pilgrimage as an image of our daily walk of faith. Now we see that it also describes our lifelong journey. Like medieval pilgrims who single-mindedly sought Jerusalem, we follow a path with a purpose. Whatever we do in life—whatever job we have, people we love, or activities we pursue—we know that all our steps are leading us to a glorious destination.

The Israelites' journey can also be called a pilgrimage, reminding us that our path has biblical as well as medieval roots. The author of Hebrews says of the Israelites (along with other Old Testament heroes),

> All these people were still living by faith when they died. They did not receive the things promised; they only saw them and welcomed them from a distance, admitting that they were foreigners and strangers [*peregrini et hospites*] on earth. (Heb 11:13)

Although often translated as "strangers" or "foreigners," *peregrini* also means "pilgrims." In this verse, the term describes people who are just passing through. The Israelites did not think of the world as their true home; they were en route to a better place. The author of Hebrews calls their pilgrimage a journey of faith and notes that God rewarded them by preparing a city for them. He not only gave them Jericho. He also built the heavenly city to which we, too, journey throughout our life.

Taking another look at the exodus route on the Hereford Map, we can see why pilgrims would be called strangers on the earth. The journey of life may have a purpose, but it also has loops and turns, switchbacks and setbacks. It crosses a formidable sea only to lead into the desert. Taking this journey, we might easily feel, with the Israelites, that we are exiles in a hostile world. We hope against hope that a better home awaits us.

I am convinced that this is why the makers of the Hereford Map plotted the exodus route in ink. They wanted Christians to follow the Israelites and so to have personal involvement in their journey. In the crazy loops and turns of the Israelites' trek, we are meant to see our own pilgrimage of life. And in the trek's endpoint, we are given a dose of encouragement to stay the road. Keeping the promised land in sight, we gain the courage to cross the sea. Go into the desert. Wander for a lifetime. Arrive home.

Sailing to Salvation

In a different part of the Hereford Map, another traveler crosses another sea. He is Odysseus, the long-suffering hero of Homer's epic poem *The Odyssey*. Following the Trojan War, the story goes, Odysseus spent ten years trying to sail home to Ithaca. He is "heartsick to glimpse even a wisp of smoke from his own chimneys," affirms the goddess Athena at the beginning of the poem.[2] As it unfolds on the map, Odysseus's tale gives us another story of traveling, wandering, and homecoming.

With his pagan pedigree, Odysseus at first seems an unlikely candidate to help Christians trying to make their own way home. Because of his personal heroism, however, the Greek hero gained special status in the Christian world. The late classical mythographer Fulgentius said that Odysseus's name meant "a stranger to all things."[3] Fulgentius put him in the same boat, so to speak, as that other group of strangers, the Israelites. Like them, Odysseus is a pilgrim. Like them, he has something to teach us about the journey of life.

On the Hereford Map, we can track the journey of Odysseus through the Mediterranean Sea, in the lower part of the world. His itinerary is not marked in ink, like the exodus route. We can, nevertheless, follow in his footsteps (or sail in his wake?) by island-hopping through the sea. After leaving Troy, located along the Black Sea, Odysseus's travels took him to the Lotus Eaters on the island of Menix, through the twin perils of Scylla and Charybdis, and to Calypso's Isle.

The map illustrates some of these sites with considerable charm. Scylla appears as a monstrous face with a mouth full of rocks, representing the shoals or stones that shipwrecked many a vessel. Charybdis resembles a coiled whirlpool (fig. 29).

---

2. Homer, *Odyssey*, 1.60–61, 2.

3. Quoted in Rahner, *Greek Myths*, 339.

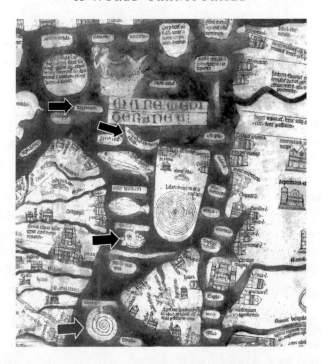

FIGURE 29. Homer's journey through the Mediterranean Sea. Detail from the Hereford Map. From bottom to top, the arrows point to Charybdis, a coiled whirlpool with a face; Scylla, with a mouth full of rocks; the island of Corfu, shaped like a boat; and Zakynthos. Note also the siren, holding a hand mirror, above Zakynthos.

Odysseus had also to resist the sirens' song. We see one of these devastating creatures at the east end of the Mediterranean Sea. She holds a hand mirror and smiles, beckoning us as she did the Greek seafarer and his crew.

After enduring these perils, Odysseus came to Corfu, home of the Phaeacians, who fashioned a boat to take him to Ithaca. On the map, Corfu assumes the shape of a small boat, representing the belief that the prow of Odysseus's ship was later turned to stone by Poseidon. Ithaca itself does not appear on the Hereford Map. However, the "woodland island" of Zakynthos, which was part of Odysseus's realm, is located above Corfu in the Mediterranean Sea (see fig. 29). Its presence on the map affirms that Odysseus finally made it home.

Odysseus's journey has resonated through the ages. In his quest to reach his homeland, he is a hero for all times. Today, we drive minivans called Odysseys and (if we are children of the 1980s) listen to Sting sing of being "caught between the Scylla and Charybdis." Some of us may have been assigned James Joyce's take on Odysseus—his novel *Ulysses*—by an ambitious college professor. Homer's imagery is woven into our life because we recognize, in his long-suffering hero, the perils we face on our journey through the world.

Medieval Christians recognized them, too. For them, Odysseus transcended his pagan pedigree to become a model for the journey of life. Like Odysseus, Christians are tossed around on the sea of life. They are shipwrecked, lured by siren songs, and beset by monsters. Odysseus shows good Christians how to overcome these setbacks and temptations and remain focused on their goal—reaching their heavenly home. "He scorns the contemplation and desire for temporal things," wrote the twelfth-century philosopher William of Conches.[4] The world and its distractions didn't matter to Odysseus; his destination did.

From Odysseus, we learn about the perseverance necessary to take the pilgrimage of life. When monsters loom in our path, we keep going. When new sights beckon, we keep going. Like Odysseus, we have problems to solve, adventures to have, romance to enjoy. These problems and pleasures are stops—islands—along our way. But we don't make the mistake of thinking of these stops as our final destination. No matter what happens, we train our sights on our heavenly home. We sail the sea until we see the smoke rising from the chimneys of our native land.

Sailing and Superhighways

Time and again, medieval Christians turned to the twin images we see on the Hereford Map: wandering the earth and crossing the sea. Just as these means of travel defined physical pilgrimage, so they came to symbolize the pilgrimage of life. Augustine of Hippo frequently describes the spiritual life as a kind of wandering. He thought that God's people were, like the Israelites, strangers on the earth. In a beautiful passage from the *Confessions*, Augustine refers to his readers as "my fellow citizens in that eternal Jerusalem, which Your pilgrim people sighs after from their Exodus, even unto their return."[5] Augustine here compares the faithful to the Israelites who walked the long and winding route that we see plotted on the Hereford Map.

4. Quoted in Chance, *Medieval Mythography*, 441.

5. Augustine, *Confessions*, 9.13.37 (Revell edition, 150). Not all translations of *The Confessions* use the term "exodus." Some choose "departure" or "pilgrimage." Augustine's

Other Christians likened the daily faith journey to the exodus. In his thirteenth-century treatise on contemplative prayer, Saint Bonaventure writes that, as we prepare to ascend to God in our mind and heart, "we shall be true Hebrews passing over from Egypt to the land promised to their fathers (Exod 13:3ff.); we shall also be Christians passing over with Christ *from this world to the Father* (John 13:1)."[6] In medieval texts and maps, the exodus served as a potent symbol for the homeward journey of life and prayer.

In 1331, the Cistercian monk Guillaume de Deguileville took up a second cartographic image in his allegorical poem *The Pilgrimage of Human Life*. The poem begins with a dream in which the narrator, Pilgrim, sees the heavenly Jerusalem as if in a mirror (fig. 30).

FIGURE 30. While sleeping, Pilgrim sees a vision of the heavenly Jerusalem, represented as a church. Miniature from a manuscript of Guillaume de Deguileville's *Pilgrimage of the Human Soul*, ca. 1430.

His vision prompts a lifelong quest to reach this sacred city. Before he sets out, Pilgrim learns the nature of his path. "You want to go to Jerusalem," his guide tells him, "and to get there you must cross the great sea. The great

---

word, *exitu*, recalls the beginning of Ps 113 in the Latin Vulgate (Ps 114 in most Protestant Bibles)—*In exitu Israel de Aegypto*—which is clearly referencing the exodus.

6. Bonaventure, *Soul's Journey into God*, 63.

sea is this world, and it is full of many troubles, tempests and torments, great storms and winds."[7] These storms and tempests bring to mind the sea journey of Odysseus. The poem's great sea even includes three Homeric monsters: Scylla (the rocks of adversity), Charybdis (the whirlpool of worldliness), and a Siren (worldly pleasure). Like Homer's epic hero, Deguileville's pilgrim faces a crossing fraught with danger. It is touch and go whether he will make it to the end.

Would it be giving too much away to tell you that he does? At the end of his life, Pilgrim arrives at the gate of the city that he saw in his vision. "You are at the gate and at the door you saw long ago in the mirror," his guide says. "If you are stripped naked you will be received within."[8] The poem is not only an admonition to stay on the straight and narrow path. It is also an encouragement. God's people can reach Jerusalem! They can defeat sin, overcome difficulties, and stay the course. They can cross the great sea.

Have you crossed any seas lately? If so, I'll warrant that it was not by means of an Odyssean sailing vessel. As travelers of the modern world, our journey looks a bit different than that of an ancient traveler or medieval pilgrim. We might be inclined to use the metaphor of a jetliner or a super-highway rather than a sea crossing to describe our trek through life. And my superhighway might look different than yours. Mine might be snarled with traffic while yours is deserted. I might drive a road full of potholes while you negotiate a sheet of ice. We might stop at different places along the way. Our pilgrimages are as different as we are from one another—as different as our faces, our dreams, and the particular struggles we encounter on our journey through life.

Yet no matter how we describe life's journey—desert, sea, superhighway—our pilgrimage paths bear a family resemblance. They involve detours and disappointments, problems and potholes. They are, sometimes, nearly impassable. No one gets a completely smooth road. We are all strangers in the world.

Most importantly, our pilgrimage roads point in the same direction. I am traveling the path that you travel, which is the same path that Augustine and the Israelites trod before us. We come from different backgrounds and pause at different places along the way, but, as Christians, we are headed to the same destination. We see it beckoning from the center of the Hereford

7. Deguileville, *Pilgrimage*, 8.
8. Ibid., 185.

Map. "At some point, early or late," Walter Wangerin Jr. writes, "at some point for all the faithful, our various ways and all our myriad faces are set upon the single most perfect ending of this earthly pilgrimage: Jerusalem."[9] One day, I'll see you there.

The Challenge for Our World

If I were to plot the pilgrimage of my life on the Hereford Map, what would it look like? Would it lead through the storm-tossed sea or the arid desert? Where would it loop, where turn? As I think about my journey, I like to imagine its pivotal points plotted in various geographical regions. The map becomes the vast landscape of my life. I see bad decisions here. Better ones there. I recall circumstances that sent me spinning all over the world. "O crooked ways!"[10] Thankfully, I also see some straighter paths: the super-highways of God's blessings. Grace. And growth.

The pilgrimage of life invites us to look back on our journey, to see where we have been and what we have experienced. The Hereford Map and some of the texts associated with it provide a rich store of metaphors to help us. We can join with medieval Christians in bemoaning the storms of life and the desertlike aridity that plagues us all from time to time. The exodus route itself is a potent symbol of the long and looping journey of life, a journey that includes some missteps but throughout which the grace of God burns steadily, like the phoenix. These metaphors don't just dress up our journey. They enable us to visualize it, as on a map, and they evoke experiences that are common to us all yet are sometimes too painful to describe in more literal terms.

This review of life has ties to a common spiritual practice called the daily examen, which asks the faithful to prayerfully consider how each day reveals the motives of the heart and God's working within it. The pilgrimage of life also reveals God's hand in our affairs, but it invites us to examine a much larger swath of time: years, decades, a lifetime. This review might involve some pain—Augustine's contrition of memory—as we bemoan, "Belatedly I loved thee, O Beauty so ancient and so new, belatedly I loved thee."[11] If we came to faith later in life, the memory of our time away from God can cut us to the heart. Even if we have been Christians from an

9. Wangerin, *This Earthly Pilgrimage*, 12.

10. Augustine, *Confessions*, 6.16.26 (Outler, 133).

11. Ibid., 10.27.38 (Outler, 224).

early age, our past may include periods of wandering that it pains us to remember. Perhaps we are wandering now.

Our pilgrimage review might also bring disappointment as we come to grips with the difficulty of our journey. "God leads none of us by the rapid and easy path to knowledge, fortune, or happiness," writes James Baldwin Brown. He adds, drawing on the metaphor of the desert, "We all of us travel by a path which has long stretches of barren and weary march, and here and there only soft resting-places, flashing like emeralds on the diadem of the desert, where we may wait and sleep and play awhile, before we gird up our loins and pursue our toilsome way."[12] Our past contains hardships, and our future holds just as many. We will never travel in a straight and uneventful line from point A to point B. As much as we might wish it, we're not going to fare better than Odysseus and the Israelites.

Yet hope blooms amidst life's crazy loops and turns. If we keep our eyes open, we might just spot the phoenix bursting into flame along our path. The desert heat that so drains us creates the perfect conditions for God's all-consuming fire. Look back, and you might see resurrection in unlooked-for places along the route of your life.

We should also keep our eyes open for what lies ahead. The pilgrimage of life may inspire us to look back, but, more importantly, it also asks us to look forward. What do we see in the distance, beyond all those loops and turns? Beyond the sea and the desert? As Christians, we see the light of Jerusalem, our true home. We see rest and peace, an end to worldly turmoil. Shining like a beacon from the center of the map, Jerusalem guides us forward. All our steps, even our missteps, will one day deliver us to its gates.

What a blessing to be able to see the end of our journey! So much of life is uncertain, so many things unknown. But one thing we do know: we will reach Jerusalem. Seeing our ending, we can claim it. We can watch ourselves move closer and closer to victory. Look at the city of Jerusalem on the Hereford Map and think for a moment about your own pilgrimage through life. Wherever you are right now—whatever loop or turn you find yourself on—you are closer to your goal than you have ever been before. Tomorrow, you will be closer still.

I confess that I hope to have many years left before I reach the gates of my heavenly home. I have children to raise. People to love. Lessons to learn. A whole life to live. As I do these things, I am getting closer to my ultimate

12. Brown, *Soul's Exodus and Pilgrimage*, 69.

goal. However long or short my journey proves to be, I am closing in on Jerusalem, closing in on Jesus. This knowledge keeps me going.

When I arrive, I won't be able to see all those missteps, those loops and wrong turns that mark my pilgrimage path. They stand out now; when I look at the map of my life, my mistakes and sufferings are sometimes all I see. One day, however, they will grow dim. Every burdensome step I have ever taken will be outshone by the light of the Lamb.

As I put one foot in front of the other, I try to lean toward the light. The sacred city of Jerusalem gives me the strength to keep going. And the Hereford Map gives me a landscape, a space, in which to visualize my journey. It helps me reframe my pilgrimage path in terms of hope rather than despair. When I look at the map, I no longer see my life as a collection of crazy loops and turns. My steps may go through the desert and cross the sea, but they do not wander aimlessly. They are taking me to my ultimate destination. Like a spiral, my journey curves inward toward a single, central point. With every step I take, I am closing in. I *will* reach Jerusalem.

Reflections and Practices

- Some of the medieval metaphors for the journey of life include loops and turns, desert wanderings, and sea crossings. How would you describe your journey through life? Which metaphors most speak to you?

- Take some time to do a pilgrimage of life review. Think about where your spiritual journey or your life journey has taken you over the years. Identify places in which the phoenix has flamed up along your path. Then spend some time in prayer. Ask God for forgiveness (and forgive yourself) for your wrong turns, thank God that he has brought you as far as he has, and ask him to take you the rest of the way home.

- Find the city of Jerusalem on the Hereford Map and picture your journey getting closer and closer to your heavenly home—to victory. Embrace your pilgrimage as one of hope.

7

Journeying through the Day

My typical day is enough to make my head spin. I don't have more to do than the average (extremely busy) person. But I have trouble switching gears between activities. When I go to pick up my youngest daughter from daycare after a writing session, for example, I fight the panic that grips me as I grip the steering wheel. Did I get enough work done? Do I have enough left in me to be fully present with my daughter for the rest of the day? When those little blue eyes meet mine, these questions fall away, and I know the joy of being with her again. Until, for one reason or another, panic sets in at a later hour. If I'm not careful, I can find myself on an emotional roller coaster as I go from hour to hour. Roller coaster is not my preferred way to travel.

In spiritual practices from the Middle Ages, I find ways to stay on an even keel as I travel through the day. Medieval Christians sanctified time. They turned the tolling of bells for work and curfew into opportunities to pray. What a great way to switch gears—prayer instead of panic! The formalized prayer practices of the Middle Ages teach modern Christians to turn to God throughout the day. We learn to see him in each ticking hour.

We get a picture of Jesus overseeing the hours in a small map from circa 1265. The map is known as the Psalter Map because it comes from a prayer book, or Psalter—the kind of book that medieval Christians used to pray the hours of the day. On this map, the face of Christ hovers over the image of the earth—an image that, given its circular shape, looks a little like the face of a clock. Its geography can teach us to tell spiritual time.

It may seem unusual to propose using this map as a clock. Don't maps measure space rather than time? Our maps do. But, as we have explored in previous chapters, time and space intertwine on maps from the medieval era. Maps describe big time—the time of the world, as we saw on the Hereford Map. They also describe small increments of time—the little hours, as some medieval prayer offices were called. The little hours matter. They are the long hours in which we care for our children. They are the short hours in which joyful times fly by. In the little hours, big things happen. Perhaps, like me, you are someone who likes to see the big picture. Maybe you wrestle with your life and find yourself asking "Why?" a good deal. Keep in mind that all life's questions, big and small, are posed and grappled with in the context of the little hours of our day—the hours that march on and on and on.

Combined with the well-known practice of fixed-hour prayer, the Psalter Map suggests a way to live out our hours. Its geography gives us a unique language to understand the places to which these crazy hours take us. And it teaches us to find Jesus in all of them. Are you ready to learn how to center each hour and experience on Jesus Christ? Let's explore the map and find Christ's face superimposed on every ticking clock we see.

Pilgrims of the Day

If you encountered any images of medieval maps before reading this book, you are likely to have seen the Psalter Map (fig. 3). Beautiful and colorful, it is reproduced not only in publications about geography but also in discussions of medieval art, thought, and religion. It has come to stand for the Middle Ages. Readers of the present book know why. Like the Hereford and Ebstorf Maps, the Psalter Map shows the world as a circle that centers on the city of Jerusalem. Jerusalem is a red dot in the middle of the earth—bull's-eye! Jesus Christ hovers in the space above the map, blessing and overseeing the world. The map thus presents a picture of the Christ-centered worldview beloved by the Middle Ages.

The map shares additional features with the Hereford and Ebstorf Maps. Earthly Paradise appears at the top of the world, with the faces of Adam and Eve. The Red Sea cuts into upper Asia. The monstrous races—fourteen of them—are lined up on the edge of Africa.

Yet the Psalter Map differs in a number of ways. It is very small, measuring only about three and a half inches in diameter. It asks to be examined closely, to be held in the hands. It isn't held much today. The Psalter Map forms one of the treasures of the British Library, where it is frequently displayed, but at a safe distance. In the Middle Ages, by contrast, this map would have been kept close to the body. It illustrated a Psalter, a book of Psalms that was used to pray the canonical hours of the day. Today, this book is called the Map Psalter.

Medieval maps frequently appeared in books. Mostly, however, they illustrated historical texts or encyclopedias, where they accompanied written descriptions of geography. The Psalter Map, by contrast, accompanied prayers. For this reason, the map has long intrigued me. We can understand a map being used to teach geography. Perhaps, if we stretch our minds, we can imagine a map hanging on a church wall. But how does a map form part of a daily regimen of prayer? How did it aid the spiritual life of its owner, and how can it help us?

It would be useful to glean information from the map's owner, but we don't know much about him or her. In the initial to Psalm 101 of the Psalter (Psalm 102 in our Bible), a monk in Benedictine garb kneels in prayer. For this reason, it is often assumed that a monk owned this little book. However, no specific individual or monastery can be assigned to it.

To find out more about the map and its use, we must rely on the context—the Psalter itself. The map appears just before the calendar, which sets out all the feast days of the church. Placed before the cycle of the months, the map reminds us that the seasons that mark the earth's turning belong to the God who made the earth. The God at the top of the map controls everything that happens on the globe—the harvest, the snows, the rains, the sun. Time belongs to him.

This includes the hours of the day. Following the calendar are the 150 Psalms of the Bible, along with some canticles (songs) and a litany to the saints. Together, these texts made up the liturgy, often called the Divine Office, that the book's owner would have recited at each canonical hour of the day. Monks prayed these hours, and so, increasingly, did people in the world. The Psalter reminded its owner to stop regularly and pray. It functioned as a user's manual for getting through the day.

The Psalter's map, too, shows us a day. Like most medieval maps, it is oriented to the east, the land of the rising sun. If we trace the outline of the map, beginning and ending at the top, we have traveled around the world—and we have also made a journey through one twenty-four-hour period. It is a little like tracing the face of a clock.

The Psalter Map thus introduces the idea of time as a journey. We travel through space and, as we saw in chapter 6, we travel through life. We also travel through the day. From the moment we arise until the next day dawns, we are on a journey. We walk with God through the hours. We cannot take this journey too carefully. Each day, each hour, is precious. How, then, should we travel?

Another image in the Map Psalter can help us. In the initial that opens Psalm 38 (Psalm 39 in our Bible), a pilgrim appears (fig. 31).

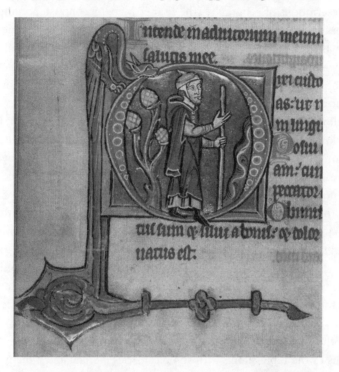

FIGURE 31. A pilgrim on the road. Historiated initial from the Map Psalter, ca. 1265. © The British Library Board, Add. MS 28681, fol. 54v.

Wearing a cloak and hat and carrying a staff, he walks to the right, as if he will soon saunter into the text of the book. His right foot, in fact, dips out of the initial and into the words of the Psalm. These words begin, "I said, 'I will watch my ways and keep my tongue from sin.'" Psalm 38 (39) is traditionally associated with the hour of matins, the night office. It sets the tone for the day that will soon dawn: watch your ways. Stay on the right path.

This little figure defines every Christian as a pilgrim of the hours. From the moment we begin our day, whether at matins or some other time, we are on a sacred journey. We're traveling with and to Jesus Christ, seeking him in each place the day takes us.

The Shape of Prayer

Medieval Christians refined a way to take a pilgrimage through the day. The Map Psalter is a prime example. As mentioned above, it contains the Psalms, canticles, and litanies that would be recited at certain hours of the day. Today, this practice is usually called fixed-hour prayer or praying the hours. Fixed-hour prayer is not a medieval invention. It originated in Jewish culture and appears as a practice of the early church in the New Testament. In Acts 3, Peter and John healed a beggar as they were on their way to three o'clock prayer—the "time of prayer," the text says—and in Acts 10, Peter went to the roof of Simon the tanner's house for noon prayer. These early prayers seem likely to have included the Psalms, which became the core of the Divine Office.

The early desert fathers, one of whose monasteries is pictured in Egypt on the Hereford Map, took up the prayer practices of the early church. They gathered at fixed times to pray the Psalms together. It is said that one group of desert monks finished one office as another group began, thus observing Paul's admonition to "pray continually" (1 Thess 5:17).

In the early Middle Ages, fixed-hour prayer became codified. The Psalms and other appropriate texts were gathered into books—Psalters—and the practice was regulated by rules. Monks gathered seven times a day to chant the Psalms; this was considered to be the centerpiece of monastic life. By the thirteenth century, fixed-hour prayer became popular among laypeople. Many individuals owned Psalters, some richly decorated, which they took to Mass or used in private devotions.

Christians today have been rediscovering the practice of fixed-hour prayer. "The hours," writes Arthur Boers, "help us live and structure our time in a way that helps us pay attention to God and God's priority throughout the day."[1] I remember the first time I structured my day in this way. The spring I was pregnant with my first child, I got a copy of Phyllis Tickle's *The Divine Hours* and followed its program. Four times a day, I stopped whatever I was doing and partly read, partly chanted, the Psalms and other readings that make up each office. This practice seemed like entering foreign territory at first. Soon, however, I began to look forward to pausing and turning my mind to God, especially when, in my daily life, I was straying too close to the edge. My spiritual anticipation began to meet the anticipation evident in my growing belly.

1. Boers, *Rhythm of God's Grace*, 6.

Fixed-hour prayer, I learned, has a good deal to do with pregnancy, for it is about expectation. Through it, we learn to expect God to show up in our day. We pause in our duties to go forth and meet him, and we know that he will be there. In pausing frequently and regularly, we also learn about our need for God, a need that never really ends. "Pray continually," Paul reminds us (1 Thess 5:17).

Prayer books and guides proliferate to help Christians "pray continually." Maps, by contrast, are rarely—or never!—seen as tools to assist with our never-ending need for prayer. Yet the Psalter Map did this very thing. It formed part of the daily prayer regimen of its owner. When the Psalter was opened in preparation for the Divine Office, its map would have been seen. Geography preceded prayer.

I believe that the map helped its owner by giving prayer a shape: its geography defined each hour as a circle with the city of Jerusalem at its center. As part of the world, the Christian stands on the outside of the circle. His job is to get to the center—to Jesus.

The map would have encouraged its owner to center on Jesus, which is just what the Divine Office aims to do. In fact, early advocates of fixed-hour prayer often associated it with important events in the life of Christ. Cyprian, a third-century bishop, said that Christians should pray in the morning to celebrate the resurrection and in the evening that Christ's light—both the light of the day and the grace of eternal light—will come again. "Christ is the true sun and the true day," writes Cyprian.[2]

Several of the hours between morning and evening came to be linked with the passion of Christ. Hippolytus, a third-century theologian, wrote,

> If you are at home, pray at the third hour [about nine o'clock] and praise God. If you are elsewhere at that time, pray in your heart to God. For in this hour Christ was seen nailed to the wood.
>
> Pray also at the sixth hour [about noon]. Because when Christ was attached to the wood of the cross, the daylight ceased and became darkness. Thus you should pray a powerful prayer at this hour, imitating the cry of him who prayed and all creation was made dark for the unbelieving Jews.
>
> Pray also at the ninth hour [about three o'clock] a great prayer with great praise, imitating the souls of the righteous who do not lie, who glorify God who remembered his saints and sent his Word to them to enlighten them. For in that hour Christ was pierced in his side, pouring out water and blood, and the rest of the time of

2. Quoted in Taft, *Liturgy of the Hours*, 20.

the day, he gave light until evening. This way he made the dawn of another day at the beginning of his sleep, fulfilling the type of his resurrection.[3]

Each canonical hour pointed to Jesus—specifically, to his crucifixion, resurrection, and the hope of his second coming. Geographically, each hour pointed to Jerusalem. As the Psalter Map's owner journeyed through the circle of the day, his prayers referred him to the center of the circle, the very center of his world. He found the Jerusalem tucked inside each hour.

If It's Three O'Clock, It Must Be Africa

Where was the Psalter's owner when he found Jerusalem in his hour of prayer? At Mass, perhaps, or in a private chapel. But where was he on his pilgrimage through the day? He could consult the Psalter's map to find out. Just as our wristwatches and cell phones give us the time, the Psalter Map functioned as a kind of clock. This "clock" didn't mark the time of day. Instead, it showed its owner the places to which he traveled in his journey through the hours. Rather than pointing to three o'clock, the Hour of None, the map pointed to Africa. Or Europe. Or Asia. Its geography defined the journey through the hours as a pilgrimage through the world. This pilgrimage included all kinds of emotional and spiritual experiences that pointed out the need for Jesus.

Let's follow the Psalter's owner on a journey around the map's geographical clock. I mentioned above that the Psalter's owner is usually assumed to be a Benedictine monk. Sometimes, however, I like to imagine the owner as someone a little like me: a woman, a wife, a mother. A Christian trying to get through the day. In the Middle Ages, well-heeled women often owned Psalters like the one described in this chapter. An example is the young woman, the "good wife," who received a domestic treatise from her new husband describing all her duties and responsibilities.[4] This woman was only fifteen years old when she married, yet, as addressed in the text, she was literate and devout. She was expected to read and to talk intelligently. She rose with a prayer on her lips and an eagerness to serve God and her husband. What if a woman like this owned the Psalter or one like

---

3. Hippolytus of Rome, *Apostolic Tradition*, chap. 41.

4. A translation of this highly entertaining text can be found in *The Good Wife's Guide*.

it? What would she have seen in the Psalter's map that helped her journey through the day?

First and foremost, this young wife saw the continent of Europe and her hometown, Paris. She saw, in other words, the place and community to which she belonged, from which she got her wealth, and in which she performed her duties. She gazed upon nearby cities to which her husband traveled in the course of his work. This corner of the world was as familiar to her as the routines of her day.

When I think about those duties and routines, I wonder about her sanity. The list of things for which this fifteen-year-old "woman" was responsible goes on and on. Entertaining guests. Exterminating fleas. Raising baby hawks. Keeping secrets. Choosing pork. Upholding the family reputation. Caring for roses in winter. Airing furs. Was she ever overwhelmed with the care of her household and a husband who was obviously exacting—exacting enough to write her a manual telling her what to do each day? It seems likely that she knew the fear of displeasing him or the bitterness of being so completely under his thumb. These fears and disappointments were the monsters in her life. They were the creatures that lived in medieval Africa.

Our housewife would never have traveled to Africa. But, being an educated woman, she might have read or heard stories about the creatures that lived there. They represented a real part of the world in which she lived, a part that was unknown, unexplored, and unsavory. The monstrous creatures resided far from the center of the world, far from safety. So, sometimes, did she. This housewife knew about life on the edge. Parts of her day took her there and trapped her in a land of fear or sin or bewilderment.

But this woman also knew the cure for monsters—the grace of God. Pausing in her day to open her Psalter and pray would have brought welcome times of respite—respite from work and from her cares and concerns. She could stop and give her world over to God. On the map, her respite was symbolized by the holiest of continents, Asia. In Asia, our housewife saw the places that marked her faith. God created man in the garden of Eden. The Israelites journeyed through the Red Sea. And in the Holy Land—at the very center of the map—Jesus died on the cross. The young wife might never be able to take a pilgrimage to Jerusalem. But she could travel there with the help of the small map in her Psalter. I imagine her taking her finger and tracing the distance between Paris and Jerusalem. She was so close— just a few inches—to Jesus!

In fact, Jesus was the one constant in her world. As her day took her to the spiritual territories pictured in Europe, Africa, and Asia, she traveled a world in which the grace of Jesus Christ shone, eternally and unchanging, from the center. She could turn to Jesus again and again throughout the long hours. He was the light in her day.

The Challenge for Our World

Like the housewife of Paris, we take our own bumpy ride through the hours. No one coasts through a perfect day. Each twenty-four-hour period brings times of familiarity, times of fear, and times of faith. As I look at the Psalter Map, I turn these times into spaces; I liken them to the three medieval continents, each with a distinctive character that helps us understand the ups and downs of our days. Europe is the land of the familiar—our everyday work and responsibilities. Africa, with its monsters, is the fearsome land. And Asia, the site of the Holy Land, is our landscape of faith. At the center of them all lies the sacred city of Jerusalem. The medieval world shown on the map does not represent the physical world we inhabit, as it did for the good wife of Paris. Instead, it sets out our spiritual world. It defines our heart's journey through the day and serves as a record of our hourly need for God's grace.

When I think about my day, I imagine traveling through the Psalter Map in a counterclockwise direction. I awake at the top of the map, in the land of the rising sun. The day is fresh: "Because of the Lord's great love we are not consumed, for his compassions never fail. They are new every morning; great is your faithfulness" (Lam 3:22–23). I groggily dedicate my day to God. Having words to do this can be a good thing, especially if one is not a morning person, so sometimes I turn to one of the Psalms historically associated with the first canonical hour of the day: "Open my lips, Lord, and my mouth will declare your praise" (Ps 51:15). This verse reminds me who is in charge of the day.

Then I go about my tasks for the day. I take care of the children and the house. Sometimes, my list of duties seems as long as that of the busy housewife of Paris (although they do not include raising hawks or airing furs; I'm not even very good at taking care of my roses in the winter). If I can, I carve out time to write. I am in my familiar corner of the world—my Europe.

Sooner or later, though, I leave this comforting place and enter an undesired land: the land of monsters. Someone will let me down. Fear will overtake me. Or perhaps I'll get impatient with the kids and turn into a monster myself. Despite my best intentions, my day always includes a journey through medieval Africa. I learn firsthand that monsters are part of the world, even a Christian's world. "Hasten, O God, to save me; come quickly, LORD, to help me" (Ps 70:1).

When I journey to monstrous territory, I have to reorient myself. Standing on the edge of the world, I turn around and face Jerusalem. When I do, I am reminded that Jesus died to defeat the monsters in my life. His victory becomes my own. I think about Jesus' hands embracing the edge of the world on the Ebstorf Map, as we examined in chapter 4, and I let Christ nudge me into the Holy Land, where I am restored by his grace. After kneeling at the foot of the cross, I am ready to keep traveling, as God wants me to do. He gives me strength so that I can continue faithfully on my journey through the day.

In this way, I travel the world in a day—several times a day, in fact. My faith is a continual journey through my Europe, my Africa, and my Asia. As I travel, I try to keep my eyes on the center of the world. Jerusalem holds my day together. Without it, the hours take on a momentum of their own. They want to take me on a roller coaster ride of emotional ups and downs: Europe, Africa, Asia! Europe, Africa, Asia! But I know how to get off this crazy ride: I train my gaze on Jerusalem. I find Jesus in each hour, each spiritual territory, that I visit.

Turning to Jesus as I circle through my day is an informal practice I have come to call "traveling the map of salvation." This practice is a little like fixed-hour prayer in that it helps us turn to God at key points in the day. During our familiar times—our Europe—we can praise God and ask him for strength and energy. When we enter monstrous territory, we turn to God in supplication: come to my aid! We then rejoice when God takes us to the Holy Land. We let him restore us so that we can continue to put one foot in front of the other.

I have found traveling the map of salvation to be ideal in my current season of life. As a mother of young children, I am alone some days only when I take a minute to duck into the bathroom. What do you do when you just don't have time to recite an office? "While most of us cannot stop work to say a prayer office seven times a day, at least thinking about the holy hours can provide a method for remembering the presence of God in daily life," writes Suzanne Guthrie.[5] I like to do more than just think about the hours, however. I like to journey through them. Traveling the map helps me quickly get a grip on my spiritual location and reminds me to look for Jesus at the center of my rapidly spinning world. Christ is my rock, and the map is my clock.

For those in a different season of life, traveling the map of salvation dovetails quite nicely with the practice of fixed-hour prayer. As we prepare to recite one of the canonical hours, for example, we can take a moment to think about where we are, spiritually speaking. Are we humming along in our duties and responsibilities? Or have we drifted into monstrous territory? Do we need God to restore us to the Holy Land? Each time we pray, whether it is the Divine Office or a spontaneous prayer of the heart, we turn our face to the sacred city of Jerusalem. Prayer is geography: it is a form of reorientation that takes us to a better place.

Let's do more than get through the day. Let's get off the roller coaster and get on the map! As we travel our world, we can be pilgrims who find the Jerusalem tucked inside each hour. When we do, the hours will never get away from us. Instead, they will be given to us as a gift, each one as precious as a bead, as round as the face of a clock, and as whole as the map of salvation.

Reflections and Practices

- If you have never attempted fixed-hour prayer, try a few simple prayers to mark certain times of the day. You might begin with morning and evening prayer, as discussed by Paul Boers, who was quoted above. You can also find prayers for morning and evening in Martin Luther's *Small Catechism*. Tickle's manuals, one of which is discussed in this chapter, include prayers for all the canonical hours of the day.

- Think about where, in terms of medieval maps, the present day has taken you. What experiences in your day have taken you to Europe? What experiences to Africa? When has God restored your soul by leading you to Asia, the landscape of grace? Use the image of the Psalter Map in figure 3 to see the circle of your day unfolding.

- As you go through the rest of your day, stop now and then to ponder where in your journey you are—Europe, Africa, or Asia. Whatever

5. Guthrie, *Praying the Hours*, 5.

you are going through, remember that Jesus centers your world, your day. Pray to your center and let Jesus take you to a better place.

8

Being Reborn

Have you been "born again"? Many Christians throw this phrase around casually, using it to mean a (preferably dramatic) conversion experience. We don't think twice when we hear believers describe themselves in this way; in fact, we may admire the story they tell about their spiritual birth. When Jesus first spoke this phrase, however, it was far more troubling than it is today. Nicodemus, the Pharisee, didn't understand it at all. After Jesus declared that "no one can see the kingdom of God unless they are born again," Nicodemus replied, "How can someone be born when they are old? . . . Surely they cannot enter a second time into their mother's womb to be born!" (John 3:3–4). He thought that Jesus meant a physical birth.

We chuckle at poor Nicodemus's naïveté. We think we know what spiritual birth is all about. But Nicodemus asked a good question. And, if he had been able to read the New Testament as we can today, he would have received a surprising answer. New Testament writers and even Jesus himself frequently linked spiritual birth with its physical counterpart. In these biblical descriptions, childbirth becomes a key component of the believer's conversion and faith.

Modern Christians often overlook these passages because, frankly, they are disturbing. Who wants to think of their faith in terms of the messy and physical process of childbirth? I glossed over the passages myself until I began studying the Middle Ages. Then I could no longer ignore them. Medieval Christians, I found, did not shy away from the New Testament metaphors of childbirth. Men and women alike embraced them as an image of their faith. And they painted an incredible picture of physical and spiritual birth on the Ebstorf Map.

This giant map, which shows the world in intimate connection with the body of Jesus, answers Nicodemus's question: What does spiritual birth really mean? Once we discover the answer, we will no longer throw around the term "born again" quite so casually! More importantly, we will see our faith as we've never seen it before. The map gives every believer a clearer understanding of their salvation, an in-depth look at divine compassion, and even—surprisingly—a new name for the savior who brought us into being.

A New Name

In chapter 4, we explored the Ebstorf Map as a compelling image of Christ's compassion. With his arms wrapped around the world, Jesus invites everyone who feels "on edge" to run to him. Let's examine this map again and find in it a new and unexpected source of compassion. Look closely at the map, especially the edge, where Jesus' head, hands, and feet appear. Jesus does not just hold the world; he embodies it. Round and full, the earth becomes his torso, from which his extremities (somewhat awkwardly) protrude. The map is actually a full-length portrait of our Lord (see fig. 2).

By contemplating Jesus' body—the creation—we learn about the creator. We see his immanence: he fills the earth with his very self. The natural wonders of the world, along with all its citizens who have ever lived, point to God's glory. We have only to open our eyes to find evidence of our creator, as Romans 1 proclaims: "For since the creation of the world God's invisible qualities—his eternal power and divine nature—have been clearly seen, being understood from what has been made, so that people are without excuse" (Rom 1:20). Like the world itself, the Ebstorf Map uses sensory perception—our experience of "what has been made"—to lead us to a greater understanding of God's nature.[1]

The map shows us a second way to understand divine creativity. Jesus' body contains the world but also swells *with* the world. To my mind—and I believe this was the intention of its makers—the Ebstorf Map pictures a pregnant body. It is round and swollen. It completely subsumes the normal proportions of the human form. And at the center of this pregnant body lies Jerusalem, which, in Jewish and Christian traditions, was often called the navel of the world. In the early fifth century, Saint Jerome wrote, "Jerusalem

1. For this interpretation of the Ebstorf Map, see Kupfer, "Reflections in the Ebstorf Map."

is situated in the middle of the earth. This is affirmed by the Prophet, showing it to be the navel of the earth, and by the psalmist expressing the birth of the lord: 'Truth,' he says, 'rose from the earth'; and next the passion: '[God] worked,' he says, 'salvation in the middle of the earth.'"[2]

Of all the names and concepts for Jerusalem that we've examined in this book—geographical center, pilgrimage destination, heavenly city—I find "navel" the most evocative. In many geographical texts, "navel" simply means "center." But of course, it also carries connotations of gestation and birth. It describes wonderfully the place of Christ's death and resurrection. In Jerusalem, Jesus gave life to the world, much as the umbilical cord carries sustenance to a new human being through the site of the navel. The city of Jerusalem signifies that our earth is forever linked, as if by an unbroken cord, to the one who carried it and brought it forth.

Together with Jesus' swollen torso, the navel gives us a new and perhaps challenging image of our Lord. We think of God as our father and Jesus himself as our friend and brother. By picturing Jesus with a pregnant body, one that delivers nourishment through the earth's navel, the Ebstorf Map presents Jesus as mother—a mother to the world. The map may have been made by the nuns in the Benedictine convent in which it was displayed. Yet its theology does not spring from a "female mind." In the Middle Ages, men of the church also thought of Jesus as a mother. This arresting tradition, so foreign to the way we address Jesus today, was quite widespread at the time the Ebstorf Map was made.

Male religious leaders frequently sought to imitate the savior's feminine side. Authority figures such as abbots and prelates saw in Jesus the nurturing and protective qualities they needed in their role as caretakers. As he lay dying, the twelfth-century Cistercian abbot Aelred of Rievaulx told his monks, "as earnestly as a mother after her sons, 'I long after you all in the bowels of Jesus Christ.'"[3] Yet Jesus' motherhood consisted of more than a set of admirable qualities; it was also physical. Abbots and monks thought about Jesus' body and the maternal nourishment it could provide. In his *Rule of Life for a Recluse*, Aelred of Rievaulx wrote,

> On your altar let it be enough for you to have a representation of
> our Savior hanging on the cross; that will bring before your mind
> his Passion for you to imitate, his outspread arms will invite you

2. Quoted in Higgins, "Defining the Earth's Center," 34. The prophet to whom Jerome refers is Ezekiel (Ezek 5:5) and the psalmist refers to Ps 74:12.

3. Quoted in Daniel, *Life of Ailred of Rievaulx*, 58.

> to embrace him, his naked breasts will feed you with the milk of
> sweetness to console you.[4]

The followers of Christ were to nurse from these breasts and so receive
spiritual food.

The Ebstorf Map represents the culmination of the medieval concep-
tion of Jesus as mother. In Aelred's passage above, Jesus lactates. On the
map, he does something even more maternal: he gives birth. It is a powerful—if, to modern eyes, sometimes uncomfortable—way of thinking about
the far-reaching compassion of Jesus. Our savior nurtures us with a body
that is neither male nor female; it is both. He gives us every part of himself,
including parts we didn't even know he had!

A Labor of Love

Would you be surprised to learn that the image of Jesus on the Ebstorf
Map has a biblical basis? The Bible contains several images of a motherly
God. In the Old Testament, God is described as a comforting mother (Isa
66:13) and a she-bear with cubs (Hos 13:8). In the New Testament, Jesus
speaks of himself as a mother hen longing to gather her chicks to her side
(Luke 13:34; Matt 23:37). Peter even likens Christ to a nursing mother in a
verse that recalls Aelred of Rievaulx's description of Jesus' lactating breasts:
"Like newborn babies, crave pure spiritual milk, so that by it you may
grow up in your salvation, now that you have tasted that the Lord is good"
(1 Pet 2:2–3).

More surprising are the New Testament passages that describe not
only a motherly God but also a birthing God. The epistle of James says, "Every good and perfect gift is from above, coming down from the Father of
the heavenly lights, who does not change like shifting shadows. He chose to
give us birth through the word of truth, that we might be a kind of firstfruits
of all he created" (Jas 1:17–18). Even though James calls God our Father, for
the act translated as "give us birth," he uses a Greek verb—*apokueō*—that,
according to Sophie Laws, "more properly denotes the female's part in giving birth."[5] Laws notes that the same verb appears in verse 15, in which
sin begets death. She believes that the repeated verb in verse 18 is meant
to heighten the contrast between sin's offspring, which is death, and God's

---

4. Aelred of Rievaulx, *Works*, 1:73.

5. Laws, *Commentary on the Epistle of James*, 75.

offspring, which is life. These differing images of birth are indeed striking. Equally arresting is the fact that James assigns to God a *physical* birthing. God is both father and mother to every person who is born again.

More remarkable still, we find in the New Testament a verse describing the childbearing experience of Jesus Christ. It is a veritable birth story. The story is told in the book of Acts, following the descent of the Holy Spirit. On this occasion, so important for the early church, Peter preached about the supremacy of Christ, proclaiming, "God raised him up, having loosed the birth pangs of death, because it was not possible for him to be held by it" (Acts 2:24). I quote this verse from a translation by Lutheran pastor Margaret Hammer, who asserts that the term "pain" or "agony" used in most Bibles today is more accurately rendered "birth pangs." Hammer writes, "The birthing imagery—unmistakable in the Greek original—is lost in most translations."[6]

Jesus' birth pangs took me by surprise (as birth pangs are wont to do). When I think of birth in connection with Jesus, I usually turn, like most Christians, to the familiar nativity passages in the Gospel of Luke, the ones that relate the coming of an infant savior. Peter's metaphor changes the game. Jesus was born of a mother yet, as Peter proclaims, became a birthing mother himself.

This metaphor, in turn, brings us to a new understanding of the crucifixion. The essential meaning of this momentous event does not change. Instead, its import is heightened. Through his choice of terms, Peter likens Jesus' agony and death to the birthing pains that presage new life. Acting as a midwife, God delivered Jesus—loosed the pangs—so that the womb opened and the world could be born anew. We often speak of Jesus' "work" on the cross. Peter's sermon helps us see that it was more than work; the cross was truly a "life-giving labor of love," in Hammer's expression.[7]

Labor and crucifixion come together on the Ebstorf Map. On this map, Jesus' hands and feet bear wounds from the cross (fig. 32).

6. Hammer, *Giving Birth*, 64.

7. Ibid., 65.

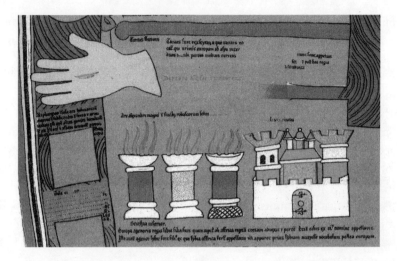

FIGURE 32. Jesus' right hand, wounded from the cross. Detail from the Ebstorf Map.

Jesus also stands in a cruciform position, his arms spread wide. The pregnant Jesus is the suffering Jesus. Together with Peter's sermon, the map gives Jesus' motherhood a precise definition: mothering means birthing. And birthing means salvation. It means grace, forgiveness, and eternal life.

The tradition of Jesus as mother is thus key for understanding our salvation. Motherhood does not just allude to Jesus' kindness and compassion. It is not a vague term describing the way that he acted. It has theological meaning that we cannot ignore. Thanks to our savior's maternal instincts, each of us receives new life. We are born into the freedom that is our birthright—literally, our birthright—in Christ.

Birth Stories

Medieval Christians responded with incredible creativity to the biblical description of Jesus' birth pangs. Two writers of the church, one an archbishop and the other a mystic, built upon the passage in Acts by visualizing the cross as a bed of labor. They poured out their devotion to the laboring Christ in two very different texts. Each one is worth reading slowly and meditating upon; each can bring us closer to Jesus and what he did for us on the cross.

The eleventh-century bishop and theologian Anselm of Canterbury wrote a "Prayer to St Paul," in which he addresses Paul as an intercessor and calls him an affectionate mother "in labour for her sons." Anselm sees Paul's motherhood as an echo of Jesus' own:

> Truly, Lord, you are a mother;
>> for both they who are in labour
>> and they who are brought forth
>>> are accepted by you.
> You have died more than they, that they may labour to bear.
>> It is by your death that they have been born,
>> for if you had not been in labour,
>>> you could not have borne death;
> and if you had not died, you would not have brought forth.
>> For, longing to bear sons into life,
>> you tasted of death,
>>> and by dying you begot them.[8]

Anselm here plays on the unusual connection between death and birth first made by Peter in the book of Acts. More prosaically, his prayer brings to mind the risks of childbirth that always have existed for mothers—sometimes, a woman dies in bringing forth her child. It is, or used to be, one of a woman's greatest fears. Jesus himself took on this fear. In accepting the humility of the cross, he accepted the humility of death in childbirth. He is the ultimate mother, dying so that his children might live.

For details on Jesus' difficult labor, we must turn to a later writer of the church, the Carthusian prioress and mystic Marguerite d'Oingt. In the early fourteenth century, Marguerite wrote *A Page of Meditations*, in which she reflects upon a vision of the Lord she received during Mass. In the course of her meditation, she considers a number of names for Jesus. In fact, Marguerite is a master of metaphor. She calls Jesus a true physician, a mirror without stain, a precious stone, a sweet electuary, and a glorious rose, among other names. When she comes to describe the passion, however, she settles, like Anselm, on the name of mother. But Anselm's poetic restraint falls away in Marguerite's meditation as she cries out to Jesus, commiserating with him on his long, thirty-three-year labor:

> Are you not my mother and more than mother? The mother who
> bore me labored at my birth for one day or one night, but you, my
> sweet and lovely Lord, were in pain for me not just one day, but

---

8. Anselm, *Prayers and Meditations*, 153.

you were in labor for more than thirty years. Oh, sweet and lovely Lord, how bitterly were you in labor for me all through your life! But when the time approached where you had to give birth, the labor was such that your holy sweat was like drops of blood which poured out of your body onto the ground.[9]

When she imagines the moment of birth, Marguerite transforms the more common meditation on the wounds of Christ into the retelling of a particularly dramatic birth story:

Oh, Sweet Lord Jesus Christ, who ever saw any mother suffer such a birth! But when the hour of the birth came you were placed on the hard bed of the cross where you could not move or turn around or stretch your limbs as someone who suffers such great pain should be able to do; and seeing this, they stretched you out and fixed you with nails and you were so stretched that there was no bone left that could still have been disjointed, and your nerves and all your veins were broken. And surely it was no wonder that your veins were broken when you gave birth to the world all in one day.[10]

In birthing the world, Jesus gave a great gift to all who live therein. He gave the gift of salvation.

Marguerite pictures this extraordinary birth using details that many women may recognize. Sweat. Blood. Shot nerves. Broken veins. She even invites us to picture Jesus lying on a bed as a woman might for part of her labor. It may stretch the devotional imagination to picture Jesus lying prostrate in labor, yet Marguerite insists upon it. She does not say that Jesus' suffering was *like* a woman's travail. In her mind, Jesus *is* a mother, one who had to go through what any mother must.

In Marguerite's vivid passage, we are invited into the delivery room and asked to witness the most difficult birth imaginable. Using imagery we may not have encountered in the context of our faith, we meditate anew on Jesus' suffering. Perhaps, in being surprised by the idea of Jesus giving birth, we are shocked out of our complacency and are able to reach new heights of compassion for what our savior went through on the cross. We cannot help being moved by this picture of a mother who would endure anything to bring new life into the world.

9. Marguerite, *Writings*, 31.
10. Ibid.

Yet this sobering account of a difficult travail goes beyond suffering. The Ebstorf Map, made around the same time that Marguerite wrote, shows us the end of the story—the joy that follows a healthy birth. On this map, Jesus not only delivers the world. He also holds it, his arms wrapped around his new creation. Having gone through labor, Jesus loves the world with the fierce and tender passion of a mother.

The Challenge for Our World

I cannot look at the Ebstorf Map or read Marguerite's text without remembering the birth of my own children. I remember the agony. The blood and sweat. The frazzled nerves. One labor was thirty-three hours in length—one hour for every year of Jesus' earthly life, I like to say. The second lasted little more than sixty minutes. Both were excruciating. Although the pain no longer wracks my body, I doubt that I will ever completely forget the physical sensation of bringing life into the world.

I know that I will never forget the sensation that followed—joy. As I held my newborn babies, my suffering fell away and I knew only the awe of becoming a mother. There was nothing I would not do for the new life in my arms. I cherish my birth stories and their mix of suffering and joy, anguish and new beginnings.

The Ebstorf Map gives me a new birth story to cherish; in this one, I become the infant so long awaited. I remember holding my babies, but the Ebstorf Map asks me to imagine being the child—the world—that Jesus holds in his nail-pierced hands. I am the one for whom he suffered. The one he loves. The one he will raise up. This birth story is written on my heart because I know that Jesus my mother will never let me go.

And not only me. Thanks to our new name for Jesus, every Christian has a birth story to tell. We may not all be mothers, but we are all children. We share a connection with our savior as intimate as the one between a mother and her newborn baby.

I suspect that in this new name, however, many of us find a challenging image of our Lord. The mothering Jesus is not the Jesus we encounter in mainstream expressions of the Christian faith. To some, this Jesus may seem more outlandish than the most fanciful fairy tale. In 2003, Dan Brown shocked the world with one such tale in which, he claimed, Jesus had married and fathered a child. *The Da Vinci Code* spawned an industry of books that refuted this fictional story point by point. The tradition of

Jesus as mother is, arguably, far more unsettling than Brown's novel. Even *The Da Vinci Code* did not go so far as to suggest that Jesus himself gave birth!

Yet this tradition, so cherished by medieval Christians, is also biblical, and it takes us to the heart of our faith. Jesus himself said that to see heaven, we must be born again. And in Acts, Peter describes that birth as Jesus' labor on the cross. To accept salvation, we must also accept Jesus as the mother who brought us forth. Savior and mother become synonymous terms.

This acceptance does not mean that we need to change all the pronouns describing Jesus to "she." It doesn't mean that we deny Christ's maleness. Medieval Christians didn't, and we shouldn't either. If we believe in the incarnation, we must hold that Jesus was born a man. His motherhood means, instead, that we take Jesus out of the box we like to keep him in. Jesus is our everything. He cannot be limited to the roles of friend, father, or brother. As our "all in all," he has to be our mother, too.

In accepting Jesus as mother, we also acknowledge something about ourselves. We are encouraged to see our faith for the birth—the painful, messy, and glorious birth—that it is. We gain a language to describe the struggle of claiming and living our life in Christ. A good example can be found in Augustine's account of his conversion in the *Confessions*. In the dramatic moments leading up to his acceptance of Jesus Christ, Augustine experienced a "fiery struggle": he made involuntary motions with his body, flung himself to the ground, and wept bitter tears. The experience sounds very physical, and it is—he is describing the birth of his faith. Afterward, Augustine says to God that he "prattled like a child to thee."[11] He was reborn and stood, childlike, before his Lord.

Each one of us goes through this birth, whether our conversion is a long process or a short and dramatic experience. Even the simple act of clinging to belief, day after day, might feel to us like a birth. Jesus saved us once and for all, but we go through the harrowing passage from doubt to faith again and again. Our faith must be reborn each day, each time we are tested, each time we lose heart.

Sometimes, our struggle is such that we ourselves seem to be giving birth, as Paul intimates in his letter to the Romans: "We know that the whole creation has been groaning as in the pains of childbirth right up to the present time. Not only so, but we ourselves, who have the firstfruits of

---

11. Augustine, *Confessions*, 9.1.1 (Outler, 179).

the Spirit, groan inwardly as we wait eagerly for our adoption to sonship, the redemption of our bodies" (Rom 8:22–23). In this passage, Paul defines the life of faith as a prolonged experience of childbirth. We imitate the creation in groaning with the painful expectation of what we are becoming. I find Paul's words to be an apt description of the suffering we endure as our redemptive selves are slowly and agonizingly born.[12] Yet however much we ourselves suffer, we must acknowledge that Jesus is the author—the mother—of our spiritual lives. He is the one who gives birth to the faith that we struggle to maintain each day.

Through all our days, Jesus never stops mothering. During each stage of our spiritual life, from our birth through our growing pains and growing maturity, he will be there. Having labored to give us life, he will complete the good work he began in us.

We can see the Ebstorf Map as an image of our spiritual life in Christ. It is a little like looking at a family album. Our life begins with gestation, as we receive nourishment through the navel of Jerusalem. The expectant savior planned for our arrival for a very long time! Next comes our birth, when Jesus gave us new life on the cross. Our life continues with our present experience, as we grow in faith and strive to walk faithfully in the world—the very world pictured as Christ's body on the map.

Through it all, Jesus never lets us go. He holds us firmly in his hands, from birth through maturation to our eventual end—which is yet another new beginning. He will see us through all our passages and tenderly guide us every step of the way. When our earthly life is over, we will meet him face to face. Our birth pains and growing pains will be no more. On that day we will rejoice, for we will be reunited with Jesus our mother. We can confidently say that in him, we will be delivered!

Reflections and Practices

- What are some of the names with which you address Jesus Christ? Which names are you most comfortable with? Which do you shy away from using?

- The Bible verses that describe a mothering God or Jesus are not often emphasized today. Take a few minutes to read a selection of these

12. For more on the Christian's experience of giving birth, see Deam, "Birth Stories."

verses: Deut 32:18, Isa 66:13, Hos 13:8, Luke 13:34, 1 Pet 2:2–3, Jas 1:17–18, and Acts 2:24.

- Pray to Jesus and try addressing him as "mother." Ask Jesus your mother to guide you through whatever growing pains you are experiencing in your life right now.

9

Being Centered

In the chapters of this book, we have learned about traveling in a Christ-centered world. Many geographical areas have taught us lessons. Europe, Africa, and Asia. North, south, east, and west. Earthly Paradise. Jerusalem. The edge.

The Hereford Map brings these lessons to life in a series of illustrations that narrate the biography of an influential historical figure—Alexander III of Macedon, known to posterity as Alexander the Great. In previous chapters, we saw references to important individuals on medieval maps, such as Augustine of Hippo, Saint Anthony, and the Greek traveler Odysseus. Most of these references are limited to a single inscription or illustration. Alexander, by contrast, receives special attention. The map mentions him by name eight times and contains an additional sixty-nine allusions to his life. The makers of the Hereford Map want us to know his full story.

It is quite a story. In the Middle Ages, as today, Alexander was both revered and reviled for conquering the world. The Hereford Map illustrates this amazing feat. It does so in a unique way, by plotting Alexander's far-ranging journeys throughout the earth. As we follow Alexander on the map, we take a tour of many of the sites we've examined throughout this book. His story is, in many ways, a summary of the greatest hits of medieval geography.

Not only that. Alexander's story also summarizes our own journey through the world. As a traveler of the Hereford Map, the conqueror had access to the same geographical sites that define our spiritual journey. The edge. The center. Earthly Paradise. Jerusalem. By tracking his travels, the map shows us how one individual, one talented but fallible man, negotiated these spiritual sites. In the process, we learn how to negotiate them, too.

Alexander is nothing if not complex. We will find in the conqueror some qualities to emulate and some to eschew. One part of his story that we definitely want to change is the ending. You may already know that, despite Alexander's remarkable achievements, his story does not play out well. As we journey through the world, we want to bring our own tale to a better conclusion! We will do so by paying close attention to sacred geography—closer, hopefully, than did the man from Macedonia. Through the grace of God and the example of Alexander, we will learn to successfully negotiate our monstrous, marvelous world.

Mapping Alexander the Great

More than two thousand years after his death, the world still seeks to understand Alexander the Great. As I write this chapter, the director Oliver Stone is preparing to release the fourth version of his epic film *Alexander*. It's no surprise that Stone—and the audience who will buy his film—can't let the hero go. His story has everything. Conquest. Prophecy. Romance. Betrayal. Untimely death.

In loving Alexander, modern audiences are right in style—medieval style, that is. Authors and artists of the Middle Ages produced more versions of the hero's story than Oliver Stone could ever hope to do. Like present-day producers, they remade Alexander into the hero they wanted him to be. One wonders, sifting through these versions, if any age will ever reach the kernel of the "real" Alexander the Great.

We won't even try to do that in the present chapter. Instead, we'll chase the medieval Alexander. He may not bear much resemblance to the historical figure you've read or heard about. For our purposes, however, this is a virtue. We're not after the fourth-century (BC) Alexander; we want to learn how medieval people understood this hero. We should thus be open to a tall tale or two.

The tales themselves fall into two camps. Sometimes, Alexander is touted as an example to follow. One medieval author dubs him "the king of kings, the man of men, called the prudent of the prudent by wise men because of the prominence of his excellence."[1] The fifth-century historian

1. Quoted in Kratz, *Romances of Alexander*, 98.

Orosius, by contrast, calls Alexander a "whirlpool of evils and most horrible hurricane."[2] For Orosius and others, the conqueror became an example of the folly of all human endeavors and a sign of divine judgment. Sometimes, a text holds both positions. Audiences had to carefully negotiate Alexander's story, discerning what in the hero's life to imitate and what to avoid.

The Hereford Map's version of Alexander has similarities to certain medieval tales, but it does not slavishly follow any particular text. It tells its own story and draws its own conclusions about Alexander the Great. It does so in a unique way. As I mentioned above, the map contains more than sixty sites that allude to Alexander's travels. Viewers of the map might—or might not—have connected Alexander with these place names. But what happens when we look at the sites that mention Alexander by name? We get a particular take on the Alexander legend. The map's inscriptions "do not exaggerate or moralize about Alexander's feats but simply state the facts," asserts scholar Naomi Reed Kline.[3] Yet we must not only read the map's inscriptions. We must also look to see *where* they are plotted. Using geography, the map does indeed moralize about Alexander the Great; it turns his story into a parable for the Christian world.

Let's examine the map's Alexander sites and begin to "read" this parable. First, we should note that the map does not picture Alexander himself. Instead, it illustrates sites and structures that represent his travels through the world. Most describe Alexander's military campaigns. To the north and east, for example, stand the altars that Alexander erected to mark the outermost boundaries of his campaigns. Numbering three in the east and two in the north, the altars are pictured on the map as elaborately decorated squares. On the Ebstorf Map, they appear as flaming altars. You can get a glimpse of them just below Jesus' right hand in figure 32 of the previous chapter.

If we look almost directly opposite the northern set of altars, we find Alexander's camp on the border of Asia and Africa (fig. 33).

2. Orosius, *Seven Books of History*, 3.7, 87.

3. Kline, *Maps of Medieval Thought*, 175.

FIGURE 33. In the center of the image is Alexander's tent, not far from the monstrous races on the edge of Africa. Detail from the Hereford Map.

The location of his brightly colored tent brings to mind the conqueror's subjugation of the African continent, which he effected before he turned his attention to Asia.

In the far east, near the top of the map, lie three of the Asian kingdoms that Alexander defeated. The most famous of these is the kingdom of Porus, who, together with a king named Abisares, "fought against Alexander the Great," the map declares. The map also describes two more eastern rulers who "received" Alexander, probably in defeat (fig. 34).

These sites remind us of Alexander's renown as a conqueror of the world, especially its far-flung regions. Medieval rulers sought to follow in his footsteps as they built their own empires. In the fifteenth century, Philip the Good, Duke of Burgundy, styled himself as a second Alexander the Great. He saw in the ancient conqueror a model for amassing territories and power. Philip even draped the exterior of one of his residences with tapestries of Alexander so that everyone could see the connection.

Connections continue to be drawn today, although managers rather than rulers are the people most frequently compared to Alexander the Great. Books on the "life lessons" of Alexander abound, teaching readers and leaders how to build empires in the manner of the man who conquered

FIGURE 34. Between two rivers in the lower part of the image can be seen an inscription mentioning the Kingdom of Porus and Abisares, who "fought against Alexander the Great." Three altars of Alexander are visible above. Detail from the Hereford Map.

the world. "Learning about the ideas and actions of Alexander the Great is an experience akin to drinking from the original fount of knowledge about strategy and tactics," asserts Partha Bose, an expert in business strategy. "He was in most ways not only the orginator of today's strategic and tactical practices that nations use to win wars and businesses to defeat competitors, but in applying them he also changed the way generations for almost 2,500 years have viewed and interacted with the world."[4]

Alexander certainly changed the way that medieval people viewed the world. By traveling to its farthest reaches, he helped define its boundaries, both physical and conceptual. He did so as an explorer as well as a conqueror. Numerous medieval tales tell of Alexander's journeys to exotic locales that most Europeans could only dream of visiting themselves. The Hereford Map shows us some of these sites. Adjacent to the altars Alexander erected on the world's northern rim, for example, lies the Marvelous Island, a mysterious site which, according to the map, he "did not visit without prayers and pledges." This inscription probably alludes to one of Alexander's many discoveries of new places and peoples.

4. Bose, *Alexander the Great's Art of Strategy*, 5.

Alexander's travels to the far reaches of Asia claimed the greatest hold on medieval audiences. In some tales, Alexander consulted oracular trees that predicted his future. We get a picture of Alexander consulting the oracle on the Ebstorf Map. Dressed in a simple robe and carrying no weapons, he is illustrated as a wisdom-seeker rather than a conqueror (fig. 35).

FIGURE 35. Alexander consults the oracle of the Trees of the Sun and Moon. Below, a Gymnosophist gazes at the sun. Detail from the Ebstorf Map.

Just below this scene appears a Gymnosophist, or sun-gazer, with whom Alexander had a theological discussion in some medieval stories (see fig. 35). In the popular romance known as the *History of the Battles of Alexander the Great*, the Gymnosophists asked Alexander why he went about the world "hither and yon." Alexander answered, "These causes are ruled by supreme providence alone; we are but ministers doing its will. The sea is not troubled except if the wind comes upon it. I wish to be at peace and withdraw from strife, but the ruler of my senses will not permit it."[5] This extraordinary confession marks one of the few instances in which the normally arrogant conqueror reveals the cracks in his armor.

The Hereford Map illustrates a final Alexandrian adventure. It shows that on the northern rim of Asia, between the Caspian Sea and Cape Boreum, Alexander locked up a terrifying people that threatened world security. The map's inscription reads,

> [Here are] all kinds of horrors, more than can be imagined: intolerable cold, a constant blasting wind from the mountains, which the inhabitants call "bizo." Here are exceedingly savage people who eat human flesh and drink blood, the accursed sons of Cain. The Lord used Alexander the Great to close them off, for within sight of the king an earthquake occurred, and mountains tumbled upon mountains all around them. Where there were no mountains, Alexander hemmed them in with an indestructible wall.[6]

This inscription mixes several legends. The "accursed sons of Cain" refers to the monstrous races that inhabited the edges of the medieval world; as we saw in chapter 3, these races frequently were thought to be descendants of Cain and therefore capable of all kinds of decadent behavior. But these cannibals also signify the descendants of Gog and Magog, a race that, according to the book of Revelation, will one day gather the world's nations into an army to destroy the people of God (Rev 20:7–10).

The Gog-Magog inscription lies within the cannibals' island prison, enclosed on its southern end by the crenellated wall Alexander built. It is the Hereford Map's lengthiest mention of Alexander, and it alerts us to his high status in the medieval world. Through this episode, the conqueror is allowed to play a key role in Christian history. Despite his pagan pedigree, he becomes no less than an agent of God.

The Ebstorf Map shows this exploit more dramatically. Inside their walled prison, Gog and Magog are shown barbarically feasting on

---

5. Schlauch, *Medieval Narrative*, 314.

6. Westrem, *Hereford Map*, 69. All English translations of inscriptions from the Hereford Map are taken from Westrem's book.

dismembered body parts (fig. 36). This little scene makes mankind glad that Alexander came along to tame the world.

FIGURE 36. Inside their walled prison, Gog and Magog feast on body parts. Detail from the Ebstorf Map.

Man on the Margin

The Hereford Map's Alexander inscriptions are united by a single geographical feature: they all lie in the world's outer zone, close to the edge. If we were to trace these inscriptions with our finger, we would draw an arc around roughly half the world. North, south, east—he tamed them all. His travels included the west as well. The *Battles of Alexander* notes that he visited the Pillars of Hercules at the western end of the world. According to another tale, he intended to "pass all bounds to subjugate the setting sun in war."[7]

7. Châtillon, *Alexandreis,* 175.

Alexander's preference for the world's rim makes the Hereford Map a unique telling of his tale. In other medieval stories, as well as historical record, Alexander did not just journey to the ends of the earth. He also subdued Mesopotamia, Greece, and Judea, the latter two located near the center of the medieval world. The Hereford Map, however, seems bent on keeping Alexander on the edge. He is a man on the margin.

In chapter 4, we learned that the outer zone signifies danger. It marks the end of the known world and serves as the habitat of monstrous creatures. Alexander met them fearlessly. In some medieval tales, he came face to face with the people who rode crocodiles, shown on the Hereford Map as the inhabitants of the Island of Meroë (fig. 37).

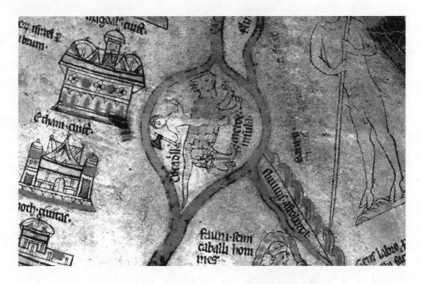

FIGURE 37. An inhabitant of Meroë rides a crocodile. Detail from the Hereford Map.

But the edge held even greater dangers. On the Hereford Map, Alexander's camp is pitched a short distance from the monstrous races that roamed the rim of medieval Africa.

Alexander's story helps us reframe the edge. It alerts us to the rewards that are born of great risk. Alexander braved the rim because it allowed him to discover new lands and peoples (even if he ended up conquering most of them). It enabled him to enlarge the boundaries of the world. The medieval Alexander was an explorer of insatiable curiosity. It was said that he plumbed the depths of the sea in a bathysphere and flew to the heavens with the aid of griffins. Along with travelers like Sir John Mandeville, he demonstrates a mindset that, in its willingness to test the limits of what is known, paved the way for the medieval world eventually to become the modern world.

Alexander's journeys teach us to expand the limits of our own world. Like the conqueror, we must take risks and push ourselves to do and be more. Discoveries are made by testing the unknown. This is true of our work, our relationships, and even our spiritual life. The Christian faith, in fact, is full of opportunities to travel beyond our comfort zone. How often do you cross this boundary? For some Christians, the spiritual disciplines present dangerously new ways to order a life lived in Jesus Christ. Perhaps reading a book on medieval world maps is a new and challenging way to think about your faith! People challenge us, too. We naturally gravitate toward our friends and other like-minded folk. Yet Jesus didn't confine himself to a cozy little small group. His "devotional life," as Hugh Halter reminds us, "happened in strange places with people we would think of as out of our comfort zones."[8] Alexander the Great encountered many outlandish creatures on his journey to the edges of the earth, but the monsters we meet might live next door. A comfort zone is nice, but sometimes we need an outer zone, too.

We shouldn't forget the dangers of the outer zone, however. Every discovery comes with its own pitfalls. Each achievement has the potential to topple us from our perch. We must find a way to carefully walk all parts of our marvelous, monstrous world.

A Parable for Our Time

How do we carefully travel the edge? We remember that our world also has a center. In the sacred city of Jerusalem, we find an anchor to which we can tether ourselves as we travel to dangerous places. This is the key lesson we learn from the Hereford Map's story of Alexander the Great. Alexander may have been a hero who braved the edge. Yet, according to the map, he became so enamored with the rim of the world that he never traveled inland. He missed the most important site the world has to offer: its center.

As we have seen, Jerusalem defines the medieval world. It reminded the map's viewers, as it reminds us, that whatever marvels might be encountered on the earth's rim, or whatever deeds accomplished there, Jesus Christ holds the central position. Only Christ makes the world safe to travel. All

8. Halter, *Sacrilege*, 127.

journeys and quests should thus pass through the sacred center. Otherwise, the danger of becoming lost on the edge becomes too great.

As a traveler of the world shown on the Hereford Map, Alexander, too, theoretically can benefit from the safety net of Jerusalem. The center belongs to him as much as to any other medieval figure. In some romances, such as the *Battles of Alexander*, the hero does go to Jerusalem. Not according to the Hereford Map, however. The map consistently shows him as far from the world's center as he could possibly be. This Alexander traveled with no net.

You can probably guess what happened next. With no center to steady him, Alexander lost his footing. He had nothing to pull him from the brink, no way to put his ambition into a larger perspective. Finally, his ambition carried him away.

According to one twelfth-century poem, the *Alexandreis*, our hero concocted a plan to sail the Nile River straight to the garden of Eden, or Earthly Paradise. The kings Porus and Abisares, whose kingdoms are plotted on the Hereford Map, were charged to provide Alexander with a fleet to take him there.

As we have seen, Earthly Paradise lies at the top, or easternmost point, of the medieval world. In planning to journey to this garden—another site on the edge—Alexander transgressed a boundary that should never be crossed: he set his sights on the one place forbidden to all humans since the gate was closed. Those around Alexander saw the folly of his misplaced ambition. In the *Alexandreis*, Alexander's men beg him to rethink his plans. Yet the conqueror proclaims, "Not to provoke the ill will of the gods, the world's too narrow, and the breadth of earth is insufficient for its only lord. But when I've passed beyond this conquered universe, I'll undertake to open to my followers another world"—by which he means Paradise itself.[9] Although an agent of God in the Gog-Magog episode, here Alexander believes himself akin to God as he prepares to lead his subjects to heaven on earth.

Not surprisingly, the deities of the *Alexandreis* do not take kindly to Alexander's transgression. The goddess Nature (a stand-in for God in the poem) calls Alexander's planned visit to Earthly Paradise a "siege," clearly believing that the mighty king means to initiate no mere tour of the garden, but an act of war. Not willing to let Alexander succeed, Nature turns to Satan for assistance. "What praise is yours, serpent, what glory, that you cast

9. Châtillon, *Alexandreis*, 166.

the first man out, if such a garden should yield its honors up to Alexander?" she taunts the lord of the underworld.[10] Satan springs into action, enlisting one of his minions to devise a plan to cut short Alexander's life. Struck down in his prime, the conqueror did not live long enough to rule the lands he held or enjoy the discoveries he made.

By illustrating Earthly Paradise, as well as the two Asian kings who were tasked to help Alexander get there, the Hereford Map gives visual form to Alexander's demise. It also reframes his fall in spiritual and geographical terms. In this cartographic narrative, Alexander is not merely an epic hero who perished before his time; he is a man who chose the edge over the center. Between these two geographical sites lies a vast space of could-have-beens: had the map's Alexander traveled, however briefly, to Jerusalem, he could have unearthed a store of humility to guide his steps. He could have abandoned his God complex in the presence of the true God. And, consequently, he could have avoided the fatal mistake of thinking that he had the power and authority to open the gates of Eden. But the Hereford Alexander did not go to Jerusalem. He gained no humility, no eternal perspective on his existence—and therefore he fell. He is a parable of a man who gains the world but loses his center.

The Challenge for Our World

When I see the figure of Alexander scurrying around the edge of the Hereford Map, I see myself. I come face to face with the conqueror within. I may not be destined to amass great lands or hold the reins of power. But I am always questing. When I take my daughter to story hour at the library, I want to be the mother who is raising the most adorable, precocious, and well-behaved child there. When I begin a new writing project, I want every word to sing (preferably on the first draft). And when I serve, I want no less than to change the world. I scurry around the edges of the earth, building my empire of achievements.

The edge can be thrilling. It is a place of promise and productivity. Sometimes, it is a place of grace. But it holds its share of monsters. Every success, however modest, tempts me to believe that I can do more, always more. I am seduced into believing, with Alexander the Great, that through my own efforts I can climb to the top of the world and pry open the gates

10. Ibid., 172.

of Paradise. I can save myself! This is a heavy burden to carry, as well as a futile one.

Thankfully, I also see, on the Hereford Map, sweet relief from this burden. I do not find relief on the edge. I find it at the center. Gleaming in the distance, Jerusalem beckons me. This city invites me to make the journey that countless pilgrims have made before me. It prompts me to leave all my *doing* and travel to the sacred center. There, I bow down before the *real* conqueror of the world. On my knees before the cross, I find rest for my questing soul.

Such rest restores me. It is good for my body, which is not made for the relentless busyness that we see in Alexander's story. No body is. Our inclination to keep going and going—to be modern-day conquerors—is so great that some Christians even speak of rest as a spiritual discipline—something to "work" on!

Real rest, however, goes beyond physical renewal. "Rest can be a spiritual act—a truly human act of submission to and dependence on God who watches over all things as we rest," writes Adele Calhoun.[11] This form of rest involves quieting our mind and our will as well as our body. When we do, we receive the blessed assurance that God is in complete control of our world. He never sleeps, never rests. Even now, he is bringing to fruition the glorious plans he set in motion at the beginning of time. I see the center—the very heart and soul—of God's plans in Jerusalem. Only there does my body stop scurrying and my mind stop scheming. Only there can I turn my world over to its creator.

Restored by the center, I am ready to face the edge again. I can slay monsters and soar to success, all while safely avoiding Earthly Paradise. I'll let Jesus open the gates of heaven when the time comes.

I go to the edge because it is part of my world—a significant part. It is where I learn, dream, and make discoveries. The edge pushes me to enlarge my thinking. Without it, my vision narrows and I sink into complacency. But I also need the center. My walk of faith includes both sites. I travel back and forth between the two in a sacred rhythm similar to the Benedictine dictum *ora et labora* (pray and work). In Alexandrian terms, we might call this dictum stillness and scurrying. Or resting and questing. This rhythm keeps me going. I can only gain strength to brave the edge if I first find rest in Jerusalem. My journey grows from the center.

11. Calhoun, *Spiritual Disciplines Handbook*, 64.

We cannot say the same of the Hereford Map's Alexander the Great. To his dying day, the man from Macedonia remained a man on the margins. Through his story, the makers of the map impart a warning for our life and times. The edge may call to us, but only Christ can center us. The world may inspire us, but only Jesus makes it safe to travel.

What incredible freedom our center gives us! We can go anywhere and be assured that, tethered to the cross, we will not fall. This is how Jesus wants us to live—freely, safely, victoriously. He wants us to soar but also to be centered. To quest but also to rest. He wants our story to have a better ending than that of Alexander. The medieval hero may have conquered the world, but through the one who loved us, we can be *more* than conquerors.

Reflections and Practices

- How does Alexander the Great live on in you? In what ways are you tempted to conquer the world?

- Look at the Hereford Map (fig. 1). Contrast the edge, where Alexander scurries around the world, with the center, where Jesus reigns. As you look at the map, meditate on Psalm 46:10: "He says, 'Be still, and know that I am God; I will be exalted among the nations, I will be exalted in the earth.'"

- In the midst of your busy day, take some time to rest in Jerusalem. Take a walk and give thanks to the creator as you admire his creation. Take a nap. Read a book. Or spend some time in worship; exalt the name of Jesus and give thanks that he is in control of your world.

- Look at your daily schedule and see if it has a healthy balance between *ora et labora*, resting and questing. If you are feeling overextended, build in some time to "be still."

CONCLUSION

Toward a Practice of Centering on Christ

Maps entertain the eye. Like other works of art, they enlighten, inform, and, in many cases, delight. They reward close looking and long attention spans. In reading this book, you have spent some time perusing maps of the Middle Ages, from their big picture to some of their smallest details. I hope they have delighted your eye.

At the same time, maps beg for action. By their very nature, they invite their users to dream and imagine, to move forward, to get up and go. When we see a map, some part of us prepares for a journey. I believe this is why medieval world maps have long frustrated scholars, who frequently castigate the maps for geographical inaccuracies that seem to render them poor traveling companions.

Yet we take journeys other than physical ones. We experience realities higher than those of earth. Even as we move forward in space, we recognize that our most important journey concerns footsteps of the heart. Medieval maps can help us with this journey. We can't fold up the Hereford Map and take it with us, but we can take it to heart as we go on our way. When we do, we find that this map not merely delights the eye, not only provides information about the medieval world and its spiritual practices. It also invites us to practice our own spirituality. It suggests ways to live that, although born in a time long past, translate to our world and the challenges we face as we move through it.

Perhaps you are an old hand at practicing your faith. Perhaps you are someone who actively seeks spiritual direction, goes on retreats, and has benefited from the spiritual disciplines. Maybe, by contrast, you yearn for more in your life with God. As we bring our study of medieval maps to a close, I want to suggest that they can lead every Christian into practices—simple but life-changing—that can renew our faith and help us live it more deeply.

A Map Full of Practices

I am a latecomer to spiritual practices, not having grown up in a church or community that engaged in them. My first encounter with such practices was a bit unorthodox. I was asked to write a review of Lauren Winner's book *Mudhouse Sabbath,* in which Winner proposes eleven practices based on a melding of her Jewish background and her Christian faith. Although Winner's book provided an unusual introduction to the topic of spiritual practices, I appreciated the way that, through these practices, she tried to reconcile her identities.

From Winner's book, I found my way to the traditional or classic disciplines, which have been part of the Christian faith for hundreds or, in some cases, thousands of years. They include such disciplines as *lectio divina.* Fixed-hour prayer. The examen of conscious. Fasting. Solitude. *Ora et labora.* Many of these practices came to my attention because they flourished in the Middle Ages, the period that captured my heart and has come to define so much of my own spirituality.

The number of Christian practices available today can seem overwhelming. Some were born centuries ago, others introduced yesterday. A look at three prominent books in the field yields more than sixty different practices![1] The fourteenth-century Augustinian mystic Walter Hilton helps us through the forest of options. His following statement concerns contemplation but can also be applied to the active life: "There can be many different ways and diverse practices leading different souls to contemplation, for there are diverse exercises in working according to people's various dispositions and the different states they are in, such as seculars and those in religious orders."[2] In other words, there is something for everyone. If you are a quiet person, there are practices for you. If you need to step outside your comfort zone, there are practices for you. Particular disciplines speak to our needs, and they might even do so at different times in our lives. Fixed-hour prayer, although I have not always been able to practice

---

1. Bass, ed., *Practicing Our Faith;* Calhoun, *Spiritual Disciplines Handbook;* and Foster, *Celebration of Discipline.*

2. Hilton, *Scale of Perfection,* 245.

it consistently, is one discipline that keeps tugging at me. I believe that it captures my need to find Christ throughout my day. I encounter all kinds of trouble when I stray too far from him.

The only real requirement for a spiritual practice, according to Walter Hilton, is that it lead us to Jesus. There may exist many kinds of practices. "Nevertheless," concludes Hilton, "there is only one gate."[3] We seek to be dead to the world and alive in Christ.

Of the various practices that I've encountered or attempted, those suggested by medieval maps have taken hold of my heart. They begin with the world, the beautiful, created world, but they never fail to lead me heavenward. These practices are summarized at the end of each chapter and described in the chapter sections titled "The Challenge for Our World." In some cases, these practices are related to the traditional Christian disciplines. The practice of "traveling the map of salvation" introduced in chapter 7, for example, has ties to fixed-hour prayer. Reviewing and celebrating our journey of life, which was discussed in chapter 6, recalls the daily examen of conscious. Mostly, however, the practices I introduce in this book stem from the maps themselves. Informed by medieval and other spiritual traditions, they are nevertheless unique to the visual experience of the Hereford Map and its companions.

Most of the practices suggested by medieval maps are reflective in nature. They lend themselves to contemplation rather than action. They can be wonderful aids for meditation on Scripture and for grasping the great truths of the Christian faith. Yet medieval maps do suggest some worthwhile exercises. As visual objects, they help us represent our thoughts spatially, almost diagrammatically. They encourage us to plot, plan, and organize our life. Chapters 2 and 7, in particular, ask us to visualize our life as a map. When first engaging in these practices, I encourage you to take out a piece of paper and draw the outline of a medieval map with its three continents (fig. 38). Don't forget to place the cross of Christ at the center!

3. Ibid.

**FIGURE 38. Drawing of a T-O map,
useful for the spiritual exercises described in this chapter.**

In chapter 2, we examined the Hereford Map as a representation of our worldview. Taking the outline of a medieval map, like that shown in figure 38, we can fill in its three continents with areas of our lives—our activities, responsibilities, goals, and so on—and see how they all revolve around Jesus Christ. This exercise reminds us that Jesus holds the central position in our lives. Nothing else, however important, can take that place. Our personal map becomes a powerful image of Jesus holding our world together.

In chapter 7, we looked at our day as a map. This time, after drawing our outline of a map, we fill in its three continents with all the places the day takes us. In this exercise, we are translating space into time—Europe represents our routines and other familiar times, Africa our fearsome times, and Asia our landscape of faith. Mapping our day, we see the cycle of emotions and experiences we go through. We travel around and around the world, sometimes at dizzying speed. Yet we aren't just "spinning our wheels." Looking to the city of Jerusalem in the middle of our map, we see that Christ steadies us; he centers every territory through which we journey. We can give our day to him.

It is just as important to see the medieval map as a representation of God's plan—the "life of God," as Dorothy Bass puts it. In chapter 3, we saw that the Hereford Map plots the whole of sacred history, from the garden of Eden to the Last Judgment. It is a worthwhile exercise to trace this history on the map itself. Looking at a reproduction of the Hereford Map, we move from the creation (at the top of the map) to the birth of sin (at the edge) to salvation (at the center) and finally to the end of time, which takes us back to the top. When we plot these key points in time, we get a summary of sacred history, a kind of diagram of God's grand design for the world. If we go a step further and imagine ourselves into the map, as medieval Christians did, we see that we have a place in God's plan. We are part of the redemption of creation.

Here, then, are three exercises to help visualize God's life and our own. If you do these exercises a few times, you will soon find that you carry around a mental image of a medieval map. It can be a blueprint for the kind of Christ-centered life you want to live. When I am having trouble in my day, or when doubt threatens my faith, the Hereford Map flashes onto the screen of my mind like a slide in an art history class. It shines into my darkness and guides me forward. I use this slide, this mental map, to think about where I am in my world and, more importantly, where Jesus is. Sometimes I find myself making a pilgrimage to him. Sometimes I cry out to him as my mother. Sometimes I need to take a hard look at my faith and remind myself who created the world, who will bring it to perfection, and who centers it in the here and now.

What Walter Hilton said of the traditional Christian practices is true of the mapping practices described in this book. There is something for everyone, something for every disposition and each experience we go through. Take a moment and review the reflections and practices summarized at the end of each chapter. Which ones speak to you the most? How do you need to find Jesus today? Do you need him to meet you on the edge and gather you into his arms? Do you need to pause in your questing and rest in him? Do you need to find yourself in the grand vision of history that he centers? Whatever your need, let yourself be drawn into a practice or reflection that takes you to the heart of your seeking soul.

The Practice of Centering on Christ

The practices and reflections described in this book lead to an overarching practice that we can call "centering on Christ." This practice comes from the most important geographical feature of medieval maps—their placement of Jerusalem at the center of the world. Again and again, these maps draw our gaze to Jerusalem. You cannot look at the Hereford Map for long without your eye coming to rest on the cross of Christ. I have tried! The map is full of sites and delights, yet Jerusalem always captures and holds my gaze. Such is the power of the center.

For this reason, I often think of medieval maps in conjunction with an important admonition from the book of Hebrews. Encouraging God's people to hold fast to their faith, the author of Hebrews writes,

> Therefore, since we are surrounded by such a great cloud of witnesses, let us throw off everything that hinders and the sin that so easily entangles. And let us run with perseverance the race marked out for us, fixing our eyes on Jesus, the pioneer and perfecter of faith. (Heb 12:1–2)

In this passage, the author of Hebrews gives a direct command to the followers of Christ. In all things, fix your eyes on Jesus. When you grow weary, fixate on him. When you become entangled in sin, fixate on him. When you can't fix your world, fixate on the one who can.

When we contemplate the Hereford Map and let our eyes rest on the city of Jerusalem, we have put this admonition into practice. We have fixed our eyes on Jesus! From here, we cannot help contemplating Christ's primacy in the world, in history, and in our lives. We magnify the name of the Lord. And, hopefully, we throw off sin, run the race, and persevere.

Fixing our eyes on Jesus is what medieval maps are all about. When I lead spiritual formation workshops on these maps, I often end by giving participants permission to forget all the details they just learned about maps and the Middle Ages. That's a little tough for a former professor to do. It's also a little tongue in cheek. After spending several hours leading people through the maps, I would prefer that they retain at least some of the information I imparted! What I really want my fellow Christians to remember, however, is the truth that Jesus centers their world. I am careful not to misuse the maps. I always acknowledge, to myself and others, that they are historical objects in their own right, as worthy of study as any other work of art. As an historian, I could never deny their intrinsic value. But as a Christian, I also find them invaluable tools for focusing on Jesus and living out the Gospel. I believe that this was the intention of the maps' makers and users, of the entire culture that produced them.

And live out the Gospel we must. Medieval maps are wonderful to peruse while sitting in a comfortable armchair—my favorite one graces the coffee shop where I wrote most of this book—but ultimately we must put their lessons into practice. We must take the maps with us as we live our lives—as we work and pray, struggle, doubt, and make mistakes. As we take our journey of faith, we can get into the habit of carrying with us the image of a Christ-centered map. This is itself a medieval idea. Saint Bonaventure wrote that within each person lies an interior Jerusalem. Our job is to seek it, find it, reach it. Our faith is a map with the cross of Christ at its center.

When we travel with this map, we find a practice in both senses of the word. I once asked a young law school graduate for an update on his life, and he replied that he was practicing law. "When are you going to do it for real?" I asked. It's an old joke, but at the time, I thought I had made a very witty remark. I now realize that it also applies to our spiritual life. We will rehearse centering on Christ all the days of our lives. We won't "get it right," *exactly* right, until we reach the end of our road. We embark on what Eugene Peterson calls, borrowing a phrase from Friedrich Nietzsche, "a long obedience in the same direction."

Centering on Christ involves a constant reordering of our world. Let me clarify this point. In an important sense, our world doesn't need reordering at all. Jesus always reigns at the center—he never changes, never moves. But we ourselves wander. We look anywhere and everywhere for the linchpin that will hold everything together. We think that we have found the center of our life only to discover that we have been focusing somewhere else entirely—on the edge, perhaps, or another place in the world.

When this happens, we are charged, first and foremost by the Bible but also by medieval maps, to find our center once more. We need to reorder our world around Jesus Christ. This is mostly a matter of orientation. Wherever we are in the world, we simply turn around and face the sacred city of Jerusalem, the cross and the empty tomb. We worship it. We tether ourselves to it. Then we can walk rightly again—through our day and our lives, through our struggles and fears. We can go anywhere in the world knowing that we are tied to the sacred center.

All the practices discussed in this book help us anchor ourselves to the center. Each small exercise and reflection feeds into the larger practice of centering on Christ. When we trace the vision of history on the Hereford Map, as we explored in chapter 3, we tell a story that finds its center in the cross of Christ. When we journey as pilgrims, as discussed in chapters 5 and 6, we journey to Jerusalem, the center of the world. When we call Jesus our mother, the topic of chapter 8, we find ourselves encircled by the one who gave nourishment to the world through the navel that is Jerusalem.

Whichever of these centering practices speaks to you the most, know that when you engage in them, or reflect on them, you are a step further on your journey. You are fixating on Jesus and living out the Gospel. At least, you are practicing doing so!

Let us practice this all our days—and let Christ bring our rehearsal to perfection. Let us keep our eyes fixed on him and in so doing see our world transformed by grace. Transformed by history. Transformed by Jerusalem. Our journey may be difficult, but we are not cast into the world alone and unaided. We have an anchor. We have a beacon. Let us cling to it as we make our way through the loops and turns of our life, our faith, our world.

As you prepare to make your own way forward, receive this blessing. Walk faithfully, knowing who centers your world. Walk fearlessly, knowing who holds its edges. Wherever you go, may the light of Christ always shine brightly from the center of your map.

For Further Exploration

Readers wishing to delve deeper into the world of medieval maps are invited to visit my website at www.lisadeam.com, which lists links to color reproductions of the maps discussed in this book, as well as other map resources.

Readers may also wish to consult some of the books and articles described below. I have divided these into sections on medieval maps in general, the three major maps discussed in this book, and some of the primary geographical sites on the maps. These resources do not, as a rule, apply medieval maps to spiritual life today. Their focus remains factual and historical. Nevertheless, they provide a good starting point for learning more about these fascinating maps and may lead readers to make spiritual discoveries of their own.

Medieval World Maps

Good and very readable introductions include the two books in the bibliography by Evelyn Edson: *Mapping Time and Space* and *The World Map, 1300–1492*. Garfield's engaging *On the Map* places medieval maps in the larger context of map history from antiquity to the present day.

Hereford Map

For an introduction to various aspects of the map, from its contents to its physical context, see Kline, *Maps of Medieval Thought*. Harvey's book, *The Hereford World Map*, is a collection of essays that reflects current scholarly consensus on the map (and on medieval world maps in general). Some of its essays will be cited below. Westrem, *The Hereford Map*, is a particularly valuable resource since it provides color illustrations of every part of the map, translates every inscription, and provides commentary on all the map's illustrations. It is a good book for taking a leisurely, in-depth tour of the Hereford Map.

Ebstorf Map

For the Ebstorf Map, see Edson, *Mapping Time and Space*, chapter 7. Kupfer, "Reflections in the Ebstorf Map," summarizes recent scholarly interpretations of the map and introduces new ones of her own. Kupfer's writing displays a spiritual sensitivity and, in my opinion, is the scholarly article that comes the closest to helping readers see the link between world maps and the Christian faith.

Psalter Map

The tiny Psalter Map has not inspired as much commentary as the Hereford and Ebstorf Maps, perhaps because of its unusual location in a medieval psalter. On this map, see Peter Barber, "Medieval Maps of the World," in Harvey, ed., *The Hereford World Map*, 15–19, and Kline, *Maps of Medieval Thought*, 223–32. Morgan, *Early Gothic Manuscripts, 1250–1285*, cat. no. 114, 82–85, discusses the art historical and manuscript context of the map.

Jerusalem

See Alexander, "Jerusalem as the 'Omphalos' of the World"; Anna-Dorothee von den Brincken, "Jerusalem on Medieval Mappae Mundi," in Harvey, ed., *The Hereford World Map*, 355–79; and Higgins, "Defining the Earth's Center in a Medieval 'Mult-Text.'"

Earthly Paradise

For Earthly Paradise on medieval maps and in medieval thought, see Delumeau, *History of Paradise*, and Scafi, *Mapping Paradise*.

Africa

On the monstrous races, see Friedman, *Monstrous Races*, and Mittman, *Maps and Monsters*. Kline, *Maps of Medieval Thought*, 142–45, provides useful diagrams that plot the location of all the monstrous races on the Hereford Map. The history of Noah's family, which has a bearing on medieval Africa, is discussed in E. and G. Wajntraub, "Noah and His Family on Medieval Maps," in Harvey, ed., *The Hereford World Map*, 381–88.

Asia

See Paul Dean Adshead Harvey, "The Holy Land on Medieval World Maps," in Harvey, ed., *The Hereford World Map*, 243–51. I cannot resist recommending a fictional title as well; Umberto Eco's novel *Baudolino* relates the eponymous hero's adventures with the monstrous races in medieval Asia. It is a fabulous and imaginative tale of west meeting east (the largely mythical east, that is) in the Middle Ages.

Alexander the Great

See Kline, *Maps of Medieval Thought*, 165–90, with a diagram plotting the Hereford Map's Alexander sites. Alexander's position on the edge of the world becomes clear when looking at this diagram.

Illustration Credits

Figure 1. Hereford Map, ca. 1300.
Source: Hereford Cathedral. Copyright The Hereford Mappa Mundi Trust and the Dean and Chapter of Hereford Cathedral.

Figure 2. Ebstorf Map, ca. 1300.
Source: Drawn facsimile of the Ebstorf Map from Konrad Miller, *Mappae-mundi: Die ältesten Weltkarten.* Vol. 5, *Die Ebstorfkarte.* Stuttgart: J. Roth, 1896. Photograph courtesy of University Library Groningen.

Figure 3. Psalter Map, ca. 1265.
Source: The British Library, Add. MS 28681, fol. 9r. © The British Library Board.

Figure 4. Augustine of Hippo. Detail from the Hereford Map.
Source: Hereford Cathedral. Copyright The Hereford Mappa Mundi Trust and the Dean and Chapter of Hereford Cathedral.

Figure 5. City of Jerusalem. Detail from the Hereford Map.
Source: Hereford Cathedral. Copyright The Hereford Mappa Mundi Trust and the Dean and Chapter of Hereford Cathedral.

Figure 6. T-O Map, Isidore of Seville, *Etymologiae*, 1472.
Source: Kraus 13, leaf 181, Harry Ransom Center, The University of Texas at Austin.

Figure 7. City of Jerusalem. Detail from the Ebstorf Map.
Source: Miller, *Mappaemundi*, vol. 5. Photograph courtesy of University Library Groningen.

Figure 8. Justin Vining, *Welcome to the World*, 2010.
Source: Valparaiso International Center, Valparaiso, Indiana. Photograph courtesy of Justin Vining.

Figure 9. Digital reconstruction of the Hereford Map in Hereford Cathedral.
Source: Adobe® Photoshop® reconstitution by Spencer Sauter, www.spen-media.com. ©spenmedia.

Figure 10. City of Hereford. Detail from the Hereford Map.
Source: Hereford Cathedral. Copyright The Hereford Mappa Mundi Trust and the Dean and Chapter of Hereford Cathedral.

Figure 11. Earthly Paradise. Detail from the Hereford Map.
Source: Drawn facsimile of the Hereford Map from Konrad Miller, *Mappae-mundi: Die ältesten Weltkarten*. Vol. 4, *Die Herefordkarte. Mit 2 Uebersichts-karten im Text und der Herefordkarte in Farbendruck als Beilage*. Stuttgart: J. Roth, 1896. Photograph courtesy of University Library Groningen.

Figure 12. Monstrous races on the edge of medieval Africa. Detail from the Hereford Map.
Source: Hereford Cathedral. Copyright The Hereford Mappa Mundi Trust and the Dean and Chapter of Hereford Cathedral.

Figure 13. Monstrous races on the edge of medieval Africa. Detail from the Hereford Map.
Source: Hereford Cathedral. Copyright The Hereford Mappa Mundi Trust and the Dean and Chapter of Hereford Cathedral.

Figure 14. T-O map, *Fleur des Histoires*, ca. 1455.
Source: Brussels, Royal Library of Belgium, ms. 9231, fol. 281v. Copyright Royal Library of Belgium.

Figure 15. Continent of Europe. Detail from the Hereford Map.
Source: Hereford Cathedral. Copyright The Hereford Mappa Mundi Trust and the Dean and Chapter of Hereford Cathedral.

Figure 16. Last Judgment. Detail from the Hereford Map.
Source: Miller, *Mappaemundi*, vol. 4. Photograph courtesy of University Library Groningen.

Figure 17. Sciopod and Pygmies in medieval Asia. Detail from the Hereford Map.
Source: Hereford Cathedral. Copyright The Hereford Mappa Mundi Trust and the Dean and Chapter of Hereford Cathedral.

Figure 18. Astomi in medieval Asia. Detail from the Hereford Map.
Source: Hereford Cathedral. Copyright The Hereford Mappa Mundi Trust and the Dean and Chapter of Hereford Cathedral.

Figure 19. A satyr and the monasteries of Saint Anthony. Detail from the Hereford Map.
Source: Hereford Cathedral. Copyright The Hereford Mappa Mundi Trust and the Dean and Chapter of Hereford Cathedral.

Figure 20. Jesus' hand holds the edge of the world. Detail from the Ebstorf Map.
Source: Miller, *Mappaemundi*, vol. 5. Photograph courtesy of University Library Groningen.

Figure 21. Pentecost and Mission of the Apostles. Tympanum over the central portal of the Basilica of Saint Mary Magdalene in Vézelay, ca. 1132.
Source: Copyright Yves Grau via iStock.

Figure 22. Pygmies and Panotii. Detail from the tympanum over the central portal of the Basilica of Saint Mary Magdalene in Vézelay, ca. 1132.
Source: Vassil via Wikimedia Commons (public domain).

Figure 23. City of Rome. Detail from the Hereford Map.
Source: Hereford Cathedral. Copyright The Hereford Mappa Mundi Trust and the Dean and Chapter of Hereford Cathedral.

Figure 24. Church of Saint James in Compostela, Spain. Detail from the Hereford Map.
Source: Hereford Cathedral. Copyright The Hereford Mappa Mundi Trust and the Dean and Chapter of Hereford Cathedral.

Figure 25. Main entrance to the Church of the Holy Sepulcher in Jerusalem.
Source: Copyright photomaru / 123RF Stock Photo.

Figure 26. A pilgrim on the road in Spain.
Source: Copyright mohnd / 123RF Stock Photo.

Figure 27. Everyman on horseback. Detail from the Hereford Map.
Source: Hereford Cathedral. Copyright The Hereford Mappa Mundi Trust and the Dean and Chapter of Hereford Cathedral.

Figure 28. Exodus route. Detail from the Hereford Map.
Source: Hereford Cathedral. Copyright The Hereford Mappa Mundi Trust and the Dean and Chapter of Hereford Cathedral.

Figure 29. Homer's journey through the Mediterranean Sea. Detail from the Hereford Map.
Source: Hereford Cathedral. Copyright The Hereford Mappa Mundi Trust and the Dean and Chapter of Hereford Cathedral.

Figure 30. Pilgrim sees the heavenly Jerusalem in his dream, Guillaume de Deguileville, *Pilgrimage of the Human Soul*, ca. 1430.
Source: Spencer Collection, Ms. 19, fol. 7r, The New York Public Library, Astor, Lenox and Tilden Foundations.

Figure 31. A pilgrim in a historiated initial from the Map Psalter, London, ca. 1265.
Source: The British Library, Add. MS 28681, fol. 54v. © The British Library Board.

Figure 32. Right hand of Jesus with wound. Detail from the Ebstorf Map.
Source: Miller, *Mappaemundi*, vol. 5. Photograph courtesy of University Library Groningen.

Figure 33. Alexander the Great's camp. Detail from the Hereford Map.
Source: Hereford Cathedral. Copyright The Hereford Mappa Mundi Trust and the Dean and Chapter of Hereford Cathedral.

Figure 34. Altars of Alexander the Great and the Kingdom of Porus and Abisares. Detail from the Hereford Map.
Source: Hereford Cathedral. Copyright The Hereford Mappa Mundi Trust and the Dean and Chapter of Hereford Cathedral.

Figure 35. Alexander the Great consults the oracle of the Trees of the Sun and Moon; a Gymnosophist gazes at the sun. Detail from the Ebstorf Map.
Source: Miller, *Mappaemundi*, vol. 5. Photograph courtesy of University Library Groningen.

Figure 36. Gog & Magog feast on body parts. Detail from the Ebstorf Map.
Source: Miller, *Mappaemundi*, vol. 5. Photograph courtesy of University Library Groningen.

Figure 37. An inhabitant of Meroë rides a crocodile. Detail from the Hereford Map.
Source: Hereford Cathedral. Copyright The Hereford Mappa Mundi Trust and the Dean and Chapter of Hereford Cathedral.

Figure 38. Drawing of T-O Map.
Source: Copyright Lisa Deam.

Bibliography

Aelred of Rievaulx. *The Works of Aelred of Rievaulx.* Vol. 1, *Treatises; The Pastoral Prayer.* Cistercian Fathers Series 2. Spencer, MA: Cistercian Publications, 1971.

Alexander, Philip S. "Jerusalem as the 'Omphalos' of the World: On the History of a Geographical Concept." In *Jerusalem: Its Sanctity and Centrality to Judaism, Christianity, and Islam,* edited by Lee I. Levine, 104–19. New York: Continuum, 1999.

Anselm. *The Prayers and Meditations of Saint Anselm.* Translated by Benedicta Ward. New York: Penguin, 1979.

Augustine. *The City of God.* Translated by Marcus Dods. New York: Modern Library, 1950.

———. *Confessions.* Translated by Vernon J. Bourke. Fathers of the Church 21. Washington, DC: Catholic University of America Press, 1966.

———. *Confessions and Enchiridion.* Translated and edited by Albert C. Outler. Library of Christian Classics 7. Philadelphia: Westminster, 1955.

———. *The Confessions of St. Augustine: Modern English Version.* Grand Rapids: Revell, 2008.

———. *Epistulae.* Edited by A. Goldbacher. Corpus Scriptorum Ecclesiasticorum Latinorum 34:2. Vienna: Tempsky, 1898.

Barna Group. "What Women Want." *Christian Women Today,* Part 2 of 4. https://www. barna.org/culture-articles/585-christian-women-today-part-2-of-4-a-look-at-womens-lifestyles-priorities-and-time-commitments.

Bass, Dorothy C., ed. *Practicing Our Faith: A Way of Life for a Searching People.* San Francisco: Jossey-Bass, 1997.

———. *Receiving the Day: Christian Practices for Opening the Gift of Time.* San Francisco: Jossey-Bass, 2000.

Boers, Arthur Paul. *The Rhythm of God's Grace: Uncovering Morning and Evening Hours of Prayer.* Brewster, MA: Paraclete, 2003.

Bonaventure. *The Soul's Journey into God; The Tree of Life; The Life of St. Francis.* Translated by Ewert Cousins. Classics of Western Spirituality. New York: Paulist, 1978.

Bose, Partha. *Alexander the Great's Art of Strategy: The Timeless Leadership Lessons of History's Greatest Empire Builder.* New York: Gotham, 2003.

Bourgeault, Cynthia. *Centering Prayer and Inner Awakening.* Cambridge, MA: Cowley, 2004.

Brown, James Baldwin. *The Soul's Exodus and Pilgrimage.* London: Smith, Elder, 1862.

Calhoun, Adele Ahlberg. *Spiritual Disciplines Handbook: Practices That Transform Us.* Downers Grove, IL: InterVarsity, 2005.

Chadwick, Owen. *Western Asceticism: Selected Translations*. Library of Christian Classics 12. Philadelphia: Westminster, 1958.

Chance, Jane. *Medieval Mythography: From Roman North Africa to the School of Chartres, A.D. 433–1177*. Gainesville: University Press of Florida, 1994.

Chareyron, Nicole. *Pilgrims to Jerusalem in the Middle Ages*. Translated by W. Donald Wilson. New York: Columbia University Press, 2005.

Châtillon, Walter of. *The Alexandreis of Walter of Châtillon: A Twelfth-Century Epic; A Verse Translation*. Translated by David Townsend. The Middle Ages Series. Philadelphia: University of Pennsylvania Press, 1996.

Chaucer, Geoffrey. *The Canterbury Tales*. Translated and adapted by Peter Ackroyd. New York: Penguin, 2009.

Daniel, Walter. *The Life of Ailred of Rievaulx*. Translated by F. M. Powicke. Medieval Classics. New York: Thomas Nelson, 1950.

Deam, Lisa. "Birth Stories." *The Cresset: A Review of Literature, the Arts, and Public Affairs* 74 (2011) 26–32.

Deguileville, Guillaume de. *The Pilgrimage of Human Life* [Le Pèlerinage de la vie humaine]. Translated by Eugene Clasby. Garland Library of Medieval Literature 76, ser. B. New York: Garland, 1992.

Delumeau, John. *History of Paradise: The Garden of Eden in Myth and Tradition*. Translated by Matthew O'Connell. New York: Continuum, 1995.

Eco, Umberto. *Baudolino*. Translated by William Weaver. New York: Harcourt, 2002.

Edson, Evelyn. *Mapping Time and Space: How Medieval Mapmakers Viewed Their World*. British Library Studies in Map History 1. London: British Library, 1997.

———. *The World Map, 1300–1492: The Persistence of Tradition and Transformation*. Baltimore: Johns Hopkins University Press, 2007.

Foster, Richard J. *Celebration of Discipline: The Path to Spiritual Growth*. 20th anniv. ed. New York: HarperSanFrancisco, 1998.

Friedman, John Block. *The Monstrous Races in Medieval Art and Thought*. Cambridge: Harvard University Press, 1981.

Garfield, Simon. *On the Map: A Mind-Expanding Exploration of the Way the World Looks*. New York: Gotham, 2013.

The Good Wife's Guide = Le ménagier de Paris: A Medieval Household Book. Translated by Gina L. Greco and Christine M. Rose. Ithaca: Cornell University Press, 2009.

Guthrie, Suzanne. *Praying the Hours*. Cambridge, MA: Cowley, 2000.

Guyon, Madame. *A Short and Very Easy Method of Prayer; Which All Can Practice with the Greatest Facility, and Arrive in a Short Time, by Its Means, at a High Degree of Perfection*. In *Spiritual Progress, or, Instructions in the Divine Life of the Soul; From the French of Fénélon and Madame Guyon*, edited by James W. Metcalf, 225–302. New York: M. W. Dodd, 1853.

Halter, Hugh. *Sacrilege: Finding Life in the Unorthodox Ways of Jesus*. Grand Rapids: Baker, 2011.

Hammer, Margaret L. *Giving Birth: Reclaiming Biblical Metaphor for Pastoral Practice*. Louisville: Westminster John Knox, 1994.

Harvey, P. D. A., ed. *The Hereford World Map: Medieval World Maps and Their Context*. British Library Studies in the History of the Book. London: British Library, 2006.

Higgins, Iain Macleod. "Defining the Earth's Center in a Medieval 'Multi-Text': Jerusalem in *The Book of John Mandeville*." In *Text and Territory: Geographical Imagination in the European Middle Ages*, edited by Sylvia Tomasch and Sealy Gilles, 29–53. Philadelphia: University of Pennsylvania Press, 1998.

Hilton, Walter. *The Scale of Perfection*. Translated by John P. H. Clark and Rosemary Dorward. Classics of Western Spirituality. New York: Paulist, 1991.

Hippolytus of Rome. *The Apostolic Tradition of Hippolytus of Rome*. Translated by Kevin P. Edgecomb. http://www.bombaxo.com/hippolytus.html.

Homer. *The Odyssey*. Translated by Stephen Mitchell. New York: Atria, 2013.

James, Steven. *Story: Recapture the Mystery*. Grand Rapids: Revell, 2006.

Kempe, Margery. *The Book of Margery Kempe: An Abridged Translation*. Translated by Liz Herbert McAvoy. Library of Medieval Women. Cambridge: D. S. Brewer, 2003.

Kline, Naomi Reed. *Maps of Medieval Thought: The Hereford Paradigm*. Woodbridge, UK: Boydell, 2001.

Kratz, Dennis M., trans. *The Romances of Alexander*. Garland Library of Medieval Literature 64, ser. B. New York: Garland, 1991.

Kupfer, Marcia. "Reflections in the Ebstorf Map: Cartography, Theology and *dilectio speculationis*." In *Mapping Medieval Geographies: Geographical Encounters in the Latin West and Beyond, 300–1600*, edited by Keith D. Lilley, 100–126. Cambridge: Cambridge University Press, 2013.

Laws, Sophie. *A Commentary on the Epistle of James*. Harper's New Testament Commentaries. San Francisco: Harper & Row, 1980.

Luther, Martin. *Luther's Small Catechism with Explanation*. St. Louis: Concordia, 2005.

Mandeville, John. *The Travels of Sir John Mandeville: With Three Narratives in Illustration of It; The Voyage of Johannes de Plano Carpini, the Journal of Friar William de Rubruquis [and] the Journal of Friar Odoric*. Translated by Alfred W. Pollard. Library of English Classics. New York: Dover, 1964.

Marguerite, d'Oin. *The Writings of Margaret of Oingt, Medieval Prioress and Mystic (d. 1310)*. Translated by Renate Blumenfeld-Kosinski. Newburyport, MA: Focus, 1990.

Miller, Konrad. *Mappaemundi: Die ältesten Weltkarten*. Vol. 4, *Die Herefordkarte. Mit 2 Uebersichtskarten im Text und der Herefordkarte in Farbendruck als Beilage*. Stuttgart: J. Roth, 1896.

———. *Mappaemundi: Die ältesten Weltkarten*. Vol. 5, *Die Ebstorfkarte*. Stuttgart: J. Roth, 1896.

Mittman, Asa Simon. *Maps and Monsters in Medieval England*. New York: Routledge, 2006.

Morgan, Nigel. *Early Gothic Manuscripts*. Vol. 2, *1250–1285*. Survey of Manuscripts Illuminated in the British Isles 4. London: Harvey Miller, 1988.

Orosius, Paulus. *The Seven Books of History Against the Pagans*. Translated by Roy J. Deferrari. Fathers of the Church 50. Washington, DC: Catholic University of America Press, 1964.

Peterson, Eugene H. *A Long Obedience in the Same Direction: Discipleship in an Instant Society*. 2nd ed. Downers Grove, IL: InterVarsity, 2000.

Preiss, Theo. "The Christian Philosophy of History." *Journal of Religion* 30 (1950) 157–70.

Prescott, H. F. M. *Friar Felix at Large: A Fifteenth-Century Pilgrimage to the Holy Land*. Westport, CT: Greenwood, 1950.

Rahner, Hugo. *Greek Myths and Christian Mystery*. Translated by Brian Battershaw. New York: Biblo and Tannen, 1971.

Scafi, Alessandro. *Mapping Paradise: A History of Heaven on Earth*. Chicago: University of Chicago Press, 2006.

Schlauch, Margaret. *Medieval Narrative: A Book of Translations*. New York: Prentice-Hall, 1928.

Sittser, Gerald L. *Water from a Deep Well: Christian Spirituality from Early Martyrs to Modern Missionaries*. Downers Grove, IL: InterVarsity, 2007.

Sumption, Jonathan. *Pilgrimage: An Image of Mediaeval Religion*. Totowa, NJ: Rowman and Littlefield, 1976.

Taft, Robert. *The Liturgy of the Hours in East and West: The Origins of the Divine Office and Its Meaning for Today*. 2nd rev. ed. Collegeville, MN: Liturgical, 1993.

Terkla, Daniel. "The Original Placement of the Hereford *Mappa Mundi*." *Imago Mundi* 56 (2004) 131–51.

Tickle, Phyllis. *The Divine Hours: Prayers for Springtime*. New York: Doubleday, 2001.

Waddell, Helen. *The Desert Fathers: Translations from the Latin with an Introduction*. Ann Arbor: University of Michigan Press, 1957.

Wangerin, Walter, Jr. *This Earthly Pilgrimage: Tales and Observations on the Way*. Grand Rapids: Zondervan, 2003.

Webb, Diana. *Pilgrims and Pilgrimage in the Medieval West*. International Library of Historical Studies 12. London: I. B. Tauris, 1999.

Webber, Robert E. *Ancient-Future Faith: Rethinking Evangelicalism for a Postmodern World*. Grand Rapids: Baker, 1999.

Westrem, Scott D. *Broader Horizons: A Study of Johannes Witte de Hese's* Itinerarius *and Medieval Travel Narratives*. Medieval Academy Books 105. Cambridge, MA: Medieval Academy of America, 2001.

———. *The Hereford Map: A Transcription and Translation of the Legends with Commentary*. Terrarum Orbis 1. Turnhout: Brepols, 2001.

Winner, Lauren F. *Mudhouse Sabbath*. Brewster, MA: Paraclete, 2003.